Digital
day trading

Digital day trading

Moving from One
Winning Stock Position to the Next

Howard Abell

DEARBORN™
A **Kaplan Professional** Company

Editorial Director: Cynthia A. Zigmund
Managing Editor: Jack Kiburz
Interior Design: Lucy Jenkins
Cover Design: Jody Billert
Typesetting: the dotted i
SuperCharts is a registered trademark of Omega Research, Inc.

©1999 by Innergame Partners

Published by Dearborn, a Kaplan Professional Company

Printed in the United States of America

99 00 01   10 9 8 7 6 5 4 3 2 1

Library of Congress Cataloging-in-Publication Data
Abell, Howard.
    Digital day trading : moving from one winning stock position to the next / Howard Abell.
        p.   cm.
    Includes bibliographical references and index.
    ISBN 0-7931-3113-8 (hardcover)
    1. Electronic trading of securities. 2. Stocks—Data processing.
3. Investment analysis. I. Title.
HG4515.95.A23   1999
332.64′0285—dc21   99-17724
                                                                            CIP

Dearborn books are available at special quantity discounts to use as premiums and sales promotions, or for use in corporate training programs. For more information, please call the Special Sales Manager at 800-621-9621, ext. 4514, or write to Dearborn Financial Publishing, Inc., 155 North Wacker Drive, Chicago, IL 60606-1719.

Dedication

This book is dedicated to all the traders who have the courage to pursue their vision of "free enterprise."

Contents

Preface

The digital age of financial investment has arrived. Individual traders and investors can now bypass brokers and enter the formerly rarefied arena of the major Wall Street players with just a PC, strengthened by their own knowledge and trading ability. As one financial writer recently quipped, "Electronic day trading is really starting to click." In fact, trading online is fast, redefining the entire concept of individual investing. As Dave Pettit, a *Wall Street Journal* editor, noted, "The rush to go online promises to dramatically change the nature of individual investing both for the investors themselves and the businesses that cater to them." For individuals, online investing has meant a chance to take full responsibility for their finances: you execute your own trades without a broker to hold your hand. The Internet has also provided a radically cheaper way to invest.

One hundred years ago the French novelist Marcel Proust observed, "The more things change the more they remain the same." This observation is also true as it relates to trading. Whether it is done digitally or conventionally, trading is the ultimate psychological chess game based on brains, guts, and timing. Trading profits are cultivated in the rich soil of market discipline, strict money management, and strategy.

No day trading system is perfect; however, the use of one is critical for trading success. To be successful, a day trading system must be profitable, consistent, and personal. In short, it must be guarded by an overriding and all-encompassing trading strategy that takes into account the real-time characteristics of dynamic markets: debilitating emotions and ambiguous technical indicators.

The key question then is, How does the trader create a real-time profitable day trading strategy that conforms to the unique psychological and methodological needs of the individual, given the special technical and psychological demands of the arena in which he is forced to perform? Historically, books on day trading stocks offer either a survey of systems and indicators that may be used for short-term trading or a compilation of specific techniques that are presented in the abstract, a hypothetical offering at best. When the psychology of trading is introduced into the discussion, it is typically mentioned in passing or as a theoretical construct rather than as an underlying and integral aspect of any winning market approach.

Digital Day Trading: Moving from One Winning Stock Position to the Next addresses all of the above considerations in detail and goes beyond anything written to date on the subject of day trading. It presents everything you need to know to trade stocks electronically on a short-term basis, including specific charts and computer setups. It combines age-old insights about risk taking and risk management with the realization and knowledge of cutting-edge, state-of-the-art technology. It is based on my 25 years of personal day trading success, intimate knowledge of the psychology underlying profitable trading based on my previous publications (see "For Further Reading"), and my work training successful traders on and off the exchange floors as a principal of a clearing firm specializing in its own proprietary traders, as well as interviews with literally hundreds of successful short-term traders.

I believe *Digital Day Trading* builds logically on the insights of my previous books and will provide an invaluable resource for market philosophy and strategy. It also offers specific technical and tactical methods bolstered by considerations of money and risk management, which will significantly strengthen a trader's day trading performance.

Success in trading.

—Howard Abell

Acknowledgments

Many people's contributions made writing *Digital Day Trading* a deeply rewarding experience. The success of this book is a testament to their outstanding talents and fertile minds. In particular, I wish to thank Bob Koppel, friend and business partner, whose market insights prove invaluable day in, day out. Bob is a living testament to the Innergame trading method.

I wish to thank Roslyn Kolin Abell, wife and friend, for her important insights into the systems portion of *Digital Day Trading* and for her strong support throughout the years.

Finally, I would like to thank Cynthia Zigmund and the entire staff at Dearborn Financial Publishing; their ongoing commitment to, and enthusiasm for, this project are gladly acknowledged.

"**D**on't be misled into thinking that anyone can walk through our doors, sit down at a computer, click off some trades, and be profitable. Day trading is a serious business. It is a profession and like other professions it requires training and experience. Your success in day trading relies on your willingness to dedicate yourself and your abilities to learn the techniques required to be successful."

—Mark Seleznov, "Electronic Day Trading and SOES Trading"

PART ONE

Psychological and Strategic Considerations

1

The Day Trader's Advantage

"Every trader knows that market truth and practice
are visceral, not cerebral. Market wisdom, like
Samurai truth, is practical truth that can only be
utilized and realized in action. It can never reside on
the level of mere theory."

— *Robert Koppel,* The Tao of Trading

I remember, as a young stockbroker 30 years ago, watching
in awe as the New York Stock Exchange ticker struggled to
complete the record volume day on Wall Street. It took 45 minutes after the close to record the final trades of the day. Dire
warnings of electronic failure and uncleared trades abounded.
We had just witnessed the first time in history that the daily volume on the New York Stock Exchange (NYSE) had exceeded
13 million shares!

Today, as I routinely walk into a modern day stockbroker's
board room, there is no "board" of stock or commodity prices
from which the term is derived. There's not even an electronic
ticker crawling across the wall. Instead, there is row after row of
computer stations with traders, young men and women, tapping
urgently on their keyboards like Skinnerian pigeons seeking
pellets. They stare into glass monitors filled with scrolling and
flashing data from which they can enter into a world heretofore

unavailable to the general public. This is the contemporary world of the electronic day trader. He or she is someone who makes one or dozens of buys and sells in one or several stocks during the course of a day and rarely ends the day with any open position in the stocks that were traded. They end the day "flat," as professionals say. This investment strategy is the polar opposite of that of the long-term investor, who will make a commitment to a stock or several stocks or a mutual fund for months or years at a time.

As in most things, there are many levels and gradations of short-term trading just as there is variation in time intervals in long-term investing. The current state of technology and reduced commission costs allow traders to buy and sell stocks for as little as the smallest trading increment, $\frac{1}{16}$ point. Short-term traders will execute trades many times in a day, building small profits into a large payday. This form of market activity is analogous to the trading activity of so-called scalpers in the pits of the Chicago and New York commodity exchanges, or of Nasdaq market makers, who spend their day bidding and offering, making a market in the smallest practical spread. It's a trading method that requires discipline, nerve, and fast-paced response to a myriad of financial and political events as they unfold.

Modes and Methods of Day Trading

Traders can choose from several short-term trading modes and methods to realize the trading objective consistent with their own personality and ability. Different trading methods may be categorized by the price increment objective that an individual trader focuses on. For example, each additional price increment to the smallest increment, $\frac{1}{16}$ point, however, presents different challenges and requires a different set of skills.

The practical increments above $\frac{1}{16}$ are $\frac{1}{4}$ to $\frac{1}{2}$, $\frac{1}{2}$ to 1 point, 1 point to 2 points, and 2 points and above.

The market, of course, is the final determinant of the end result, but traders must focus their energies and create a method that is consistent in its objective. Switching objectives, such as making a trade for $\frac{1}{2}$ point and trying to stretch it into a 2-point trade, is doomed for failure, in my opinion, over a series of trades. Worse yet is designing a risk management system for an objective of $\frac{1}{2}$ point and then changing it to attempt to stay the course for 2 or 3 points at a time. This is no different from executing a trade that starts out as a short-term swing trade and turns into a long-term investment because the trader refuses to accept the initial loss!

It is my goal in *Digital Day Trading* to introduce you to the new and exciting world of electronic short-term stock trading and to present many of the tried and true methods that successful traders routinely employ. Many of these methods don't require you to sit in front of a computer screen every minute if you don't choose to. The technology that has accommodated the increase of volume from that record 13-million-share day of 30 years ago to the present-day average on the NYSE in excess of 500 million shares also allows you, as a day trader, to compete with market professionals on a level technological playing field.

Until the 1970s, the securities industry was conducted in its own time-honored fashion. The brokerage houses controlled the flow of orders, made largely to the NYSE but to a lesser degree to the American Stock Exchange (AMEX) and the over-the-counter (OTC) market. Not only was the order flow controlled but the commissions charged to the general public were fixed. Price reporting was available at your broker's office or in newspapers, and only professional securities traders or wealthy individuals had real-time access to price and volume information.

In 1971 the National Association of Securities Dealers created Nasdaq, an electronic market where members could display their bids and offers to other members. On May 1, 1975, fixed commissions were terminated by Securities and Exchange Commission (SEC) decree, and a new era of competitive pricing and discount brokerage was born. The termination of fixed commissions, which was the culmination of a five-year phase-out and said at the time to be the death knell of the securities industry, actually turned out to be the main ingredient in the subsequent explosion of trading volume. An industry that had predicted brokerage house failures and the end of the industry saw a new breed of brokerage house called "discount brokers" provide an increased order flow at greatly reduced prices. Not only were discount brokers profitable, but they generated the explosion in trading volume by making the cost of buying and selling an insignificant factor.

Over the years and with some SEC rules changes, the Nasdaq system has evolved from a member-only, inside market to a quotation platform open to all. In 1985 the Small Order Execution System (SOES) was introduced to allow customers to buy on the offer and sell on the bid for up to one thousand shares at a time. After the 1987 crash, when market makers refused to answer phones or backed away from their quotes, Nasdaq instituted an automatic electronic execution system through SOES. Soon after, the SelectNet system, which allowed customers to see and trade with market maker bids and offers as well as other customers' bids and offers, was created.

The final ingredient in the explosion in the securities industry was the technological advances that have occurred recently and are still occurring: online access to the markets that is readily available to all at a cheap cost with state-of-the-art quickness and precision. Today's technology offers the buying and selling of stock via the Internet, completely bypassing a broker as well as securing inexpensive online systems. These online systems not only supply quotes and news but also allow the direct entry of orders through participation in the SelectNet system and in the various electronic communications networks (ECNs) that present your bids and offers on an equal footing with other market professionals.

Online Trading

To use the concepts, patterns, and ideas in *Digital Day Trading*, traders need to familiarize themselves with electronic trading. Because the focus of this book is the specific strategies and techniques that the day trader can use to enhance market performance, I won't spend a great deal of space on the technology itself. *The Electronic Day Trader* (McGraw-Hill) and *The Online Investor* (Wiley) do that quite well rather than focus in a very comprehensive way on market strategy or specific techniques.

Online trading can mean the Internet, the World Wide Web, or any other available means of transmitting orders and information such as a private network, satellite, TV, or even pager technology. In the time between the conception of this book and writing this chapter, trading technology made extraordinary advances—from simple Internet order entry access to securities markets to electronic networks available at brokerage sites or total market access on a trader's PC.

The technologies change daily. As an example, online trading access began as a method to get delayed quotes on a PC, typing in an order to buy or sell a security, and then sending that order to a broker, who would forward it on to be executed. What ensued was the ability to obtain live quotes inexpensively, to enter orders and receive "fills" (i.e., executed orders) directly from the markets that the security trades on, and to have at your fingertips many management tools that serve to organize your portfolio and enhance money management. Following that, new-styled brokers emerged, supplying computer stations with the most advanced software and instant access to all markets via Nasdaq Level II and various ECNs, and offering information and account management tools in many cities across the nation.

Now, the same level of technology that was available at brokers' offices is available online on your PC for a reasonable fee on a fee-for-service basis. Real-time market quotes, charts, news, ticker alerts, one-button order entry, and almost instantaneous order execution are now a click away with excellent reliability.

The World of Electronic Trading

SuperDot

SuperDot is the electronic platform for listed markets. Almost 40 percent of the shares traded on the NYSE in any one day are executed on SuperDot. This system, which links member firms to the specialists on the floor of the exchange, can handle up to 99,999 orders. Although SuperDot usually is not available to individuals, several other systems offer similar access to the markets.

Electronic Communications Networks

Instinet, Island, Bloomberg, and Teranova are ECNs available to everyone. Traders, market makers, and institutions can have their bid or offers displayed and thereby make a market on Nasdaq stocks. Through ECN order entry terminals or your own PC, you can now participate in the entire Nasdaq market on an equal basis with market professionals.

At the present time the Nasdaq market offers the best opportunity for you, as a day trader, to compete. Because listed securities that are traded on the NYSE, the AMEX, and other exchanges in the United States and around the world are still traded within a specialist system, you don't have direct access to buyers and sellers and thus lose much of your edge in short-term trades. This is not to say, however, that opportunity in the listed markets is lacking. Many good trades and many interesting stocks are available for your portfolio, but you must adapt your methods to the specialist system.

In my view, it is more important to develop a consistent, disciplined approach to trading based on the information available in the market in terms of price and other statistics than worry about whether it's a specialist, a market maker, a hedge fund, or Joe Trader on the other side of your trade.

How to Begin

Hardware

Almost any computer purchased in the past two years should have the capability to put you online. The minimum requirements for online trading are Pentium or an equivalent 133 MHz, 32 RAM, 28 bps or higher modem, and 1 gigabyte or higher hard drive memory. Anything you add as an upgrade or enhancement will increase your efficiency and make your life easier.

More recent software—for example, live NYSE, AMEX, and Nasdaq quotes; Nasdaq Level II displays; live technical charts; custom studies; position manager; a point-and-click execution panel; and custom "hot" keys—may require more than the minimum essentials. If you intend to day trade actively, then a higher level of hardware is well worth the additional expense.

Software

The different categories of software are the following:

- *Internet access.* Access software is provided by an Internet service provider (ISP) and allows you to make the connection between your PC and the ISP's server.
- *Internet browser.* The two most common browsers are Microsoft and Netscape. Microsoft's Internet Explorer is included in your Microsoft PC operating system, and Netscape can be downloaded directly from the Internet.
- *Order entry software.* This software is provided by the brokerage company that holds your account. Along with sending orders and receiving fills, it may keep track of your trades; show you your portfolio; and provide quotes, news, charts, market maker screens, tickers, and supply research reports.

Analysis software. Many software choices contain various technical studies or allow you to create your own. Some of this software also allows you to test what you create or test a combination of studies that are included in the software. The product manufacturers and vendors, who are actively soliciting your business, make finding and getting acquainted with your requirements easier. Pick up any business newspaper or magazine, or turn on a local or national financial news station on radio or TV, and you'll find an enormous choice. Some examples of this software are Trade Station by Omega Research, MetaStock by Equis, TeleChart by Worden Brothers, Inc., and Trading Expert Pro by AIQ.

Setting Up a Business Plan

As with any business, content and substance, not wishful thinking, are called for. Write a business plan that contains the following:

- A clear statement of your business goals and philosophy
- A list of resources available now and in the future to pursue a day trading business
- Specific plans for the business—a description of your proprietary ideas, strategies, and tactics for advancing your goals
- A projected cash flow worksheet with a balance sheet that precisely presents your current financial position
- Identification of an ongoing mechanism for evaluation and future testing

With the electronic system in place, your business plan completed, and the costs to do business well calculated, what is needed next is to understand how to take full advantage of the contemporary marketplace.

To decide where to focus your energies, it is essential to understand the various categories of day traders and how they differ. Ultimately, time and personality should determine your specific market approach.

Categories of Traders

Following are the various categories of day traders:

- Scalpers
- Market makers

- Quick-turn traders
- Swing traders

Scalpers. Scalping is the most active method of trading and requires real-time access to the markets. The scalper takes a position and immediately bids or offers his position at $\frac{1}{16}$, $\frac{1}{8}$, or $\frac{1}{4}$ point above or below the market, hoping to take a small profit. If he can repeat this 20 or 30 times a day, he will end each day with a sizable gain. The advantage of scalping is the ability to control losses if traders are disciplined and quick. This trading method requires total focus and a minute-to-minute commitment to the market.

Market makers. Although not as active or intense as scalping, market making requires a total commitment to the market. The trader attempts to buy on the bid and sell on the offer along with the professional market makers. The bid and offer spreads that this trader is working with are usually larger than scalpers' spreads and, depending on the stock, could be from $\frac{1}{4}$ point to 1 point.

To trade effectively, scalpers or market makers need to purchase the necessary computer hardware and software that will support an order entry system or, for optimum effectiveness, they need a Nasdaq Level II, which provides bids and offers as well as the depth of the market. Or they can become associated with one of several securities firms specializing in electronic day trading. Either way I recommend an extensive training period before you attempt to trade actively as a scalper or market maker.

Choosing the right firm to hold your account is your first important trading decision. If you intend to be a scalper day trader, a good firm will have a training process in place and give you access to an individual responsible for ensuring that you have the necessary skills to trade on the electronic communications network. These skills include setting up your trading screen so that you can see the markets of your choice; understanding how and what orders are available to you and how to enter those orders so that what you intend to do is what in fact occurs; practicing entering orders not only for accuracy but for speed; and having all the pertinent information on your screen that is available. If your goal is to day trade online, then many of the established firms can meet your needs. Firms such as Charles Schwab or e-trade make it easy to get connected.

The scalper and market maker style of trading requires getting in and out of positions very quickly and keeping the size of losing trades to a minimum. Traders may watch many of the most actively traded stocks and, when sensing movement or a trend developing, jump into that stock hoping to profit by $\frac{1}{8}$ or $\frac{1}{4}$ point. If the trade doesn't develop immediately, traders may sell for $\frac{1}{16}$ point or for a "scratch" (selling for the same price as the purchase) or take a small loss. They realize one very important fact: Another trade will be along any moment and success means keeping the losing trades small.

Quick-turn traders. I differentiate the scalper and market maker from the day trader who, unlike them, is aware of and capitalizes on market direction. Where scalpers or market makers may be aware of a directional bias to the market they are trading, it is not their primary focus. In contrast, the quick-turn day trader is highly concentrated on market action and studies the sequence of bids and offers to enter the market at a time when he or she feels a move of $\frac{1}{2}$ to 1 point is about to occur. This day trader may pay $\frac{1}{16}$ or $\frac{1}{8}$ point to get into a moving stock and will also sell out of his or her position just moments later if his or her price objective is realized.

Swing traders. Swing traders are fundamentally concerned with market direction. They attempt to trade specific market patterns that allow for circumscribed risk where the profit potential is from 1 to 3 or more points in a day. I think this type of trading takes more time to develop and has a wider price and time horizon so that many more of us can successfully use it and thus avoid a minute-by-minute focus on the market or computer screen.

Position traders. The day trade position trader tries to accumulate a multiple position in a stock to take advantage of a larger daily or two- to three-day market move. This is an aggressive trading style that usually requires more capital than the other categories.

The discussion of trading philosophy and strategy that follows throughout *Digital Day Trading* concentrates on the last three day trading categories discussed, namely, quick-turn trading, swing trading, and short-term position trading. The specific method and patterns I describe have been thoroughly tested and widely used with successful results over my long-term day trading career. In addition, I have included techniques that were shared with me by proprietary and institutional traders as well as floor traders whose record of success I know of firsthand.

Before we look at specific setups, it is important to clearly understand the strategies and psychological factors that in the final analysis are the ultimate key to market success. As the Chinese philosopher Lao-tzu observed: "He who knows much about others may be learned, but he who understands himself is more intelligent. He who controls others may be more powerful, but he who has mastered himself is mightier still."

2

The Psychology of Successful Day Trading

In Bernard Baruch's autobiography *Baruch: My Own Story* (Holt, Rinehart & Winston, 1957), the legendary entrepreneur offers ten rules for successful speculation:

1. Don't speculate unless you do it full-time.
2. Resist so-called inside information or tips.
3. Before purchasing a security, know everything you can find out about the issuing company, especially its earnings and capacity for growth.
4. Never attempt to buy a bottom or sell a top of a market: this is a feat achieved only by liars.
5. Take your losses swiftly and clearly; the first loss is your easiest.
6. Don't buy too many securities; focus on a few investments that can be monitored carefully.

7. Periodically reappraise all your investments to make sure they are appropriate to your particular strategy.
8. Know when you can sell to your greatest advantage (of course, this also applies to buying).
9. Never invest all your funds; keep liquid.
10. Don't try to be a jack of all investments; stick to the field you know best.

Baruch, who was a lifelong skeptic of both giving and taking advice, qualified his rules of sound speculation with the following caveat: "Being so skeptical about the usefulness of advice, I have been reluctant to lay down any rules or guidelines on how to invest or speculate wisely. Still, there are a number of things I have learned from my own experience which might be worth listing for those who are able to muster the necessary self-discipline." And, of course, isn't that the essence of it? All rules of sound investment begin and end with the adoption and mastery of specific psychological skills that successful trading requires.

Day trading, in particular, because of the very nature of short-term trading, forces us to sink or swim in our own psychology. It is the concentrated time frame of split-second decision making within a context—perhaps barrage is a better word—of conflicting and contradictory data that makes it seem at times impossible! Not so.

In my experience day trading can be enormously rewarding both psychologically and financially. But only if the right attitudes are put in place and the necessary psychological skills are mastered.

The Psychological Skills Necessary to Become a Successful Day Trader

The necessary psychological skills for day trading are these:

* Compelling personal motivation
* Goal setting
* Confidence
* Anxiety control
* Focus
* State of mind management

Compelling Motivation

Compelling motivation involves possessing the intensity to do whatever it takes to win at trading: to overcome a bad day or a temporary setback in the market in order to achieve your trading goals. It also means sticking to your trading plan and not allowing a momentary impulse based on fear and greed to control your decisions. Many day traders live and die on a roller coaster of inhibiting emotion. This is not the soil in which effective trading flowers.

Goal Setting

Goal setting is key for traders. It focuses them on what is important in terms of motivation, outcome, and mechanics. Goals give direction and focus to the trading plan as well. You must know what you are trying to accomplish if you want to achieve an excellent trading result. You must be able to answer without qualification: Am I scalping, quick-turn trading, or swing trading? Is my time frame 5 minutes, 30 minutes, or five days? Then you must act according to your answers. Goal setting allows you to make decisions without hesitation or ambiguity.

The Importance of Day Trading Goals

Goal	*Benefit*	*Trading Behavior*
Performance goal	Improvement of your own standards	Increase in physical and psychological skills related to trading
Outcome goal	Helps determine what's important to you	Development of techniques and strategies that match your personality
Motivation goal	Helps increase effort Directs attention	Increase in enthusiasm and confidence

Ask yourself the following questions:

- Do I have a clearly defined set of trading goals in writing?
- Have I specifically done something to move me closer to achieving my goals?
- Do I have a clear idea of what I want to accomplish right now in the market?
- Do I concentrate on goals rather than procedures?
- Do I evaluate my progress based on accomplishment rather than activity?

As you think about your trading goals, remember that they should satisfy the following criteria. Your trading goals should be *specific*—that is, clear, precise, and well defined. They should be *time framed*—that is, stated within a specific time period. Your goals should be *positive*—that is, stated in a way that is empowering. They should be *controlled*—in other words, your goals should be completely within your control. They should be *realistic*—it's not necessary to became the next George Soros . . . that was George's goal! And finally, your goals should be *measurable*—that is, easily quantifiable.

From the experience of training my own proprietary traders, I have found that when traders abandon their goals, it is because they suffer from one of the following weaknesses:

- Self-limiting beliefs
- An unresourceful state of mind
- Poor focus
- An ill-defined personal trading strategy
- A lack of physical and psychological energy

The solution to overcoming these trading obstacles always resides in psychological rather than technical analysis—but of course you already know this!

Confidence

When I speak of confidence, I'm not referring to cockiness, euphoria, or arrogance. Hubris in trading is lethal. Confidence, on the other hand, is essential and is the trader's natural expression of self-trust and being in control. It is effortlessly expecting a good result based on hard work, discipline, and an effective (tested and proven) methodology.

Anxiety Control

Sometimes I think anxiety was invented just for trading! There are so many anxieties the trader has to confront and master to be effective and apply his proven strategy.

Day trading anxiety stems from a variety of sources. Fear of failure is perhaps chief among them, manifesting itself in traders' feelings of intense pressure to perform well. And traders' self-worth is often tied to their trading. Then there are perfectionist traders concerned about what others think. For overcoming—or at least minimizing—perfectionism, traders should focus on applying their methodology, mentally rehearse the mechanics of the trade, and convince themselves that trading is not about proving anything to anybody. If you are a perfectionist, the more you focus on your methodology, the more you'll feel in control of your anxiety.

Another source of trading anxiety is fear of success. Traders may lose control and engage in euphoric trading, while in fact doubting themselves. If your day trading approach has shown statistical reliability in its performance, rehearse feelings of confidence as you mentally run through the placement, follow through, and close out the trade. Feel in a literal sense how you personally experience confidence.

Finally, some traders are anxious about losing control, feeling the market is out to get them (it's not!). These traders lose their sense of personal responsibility when trading and must teach themselves how to get into a physically and psychologically relaxed state when trading. If you fear losing control, focus on your specific methodology and expect small losses!

Focus

The following reveals graphically the focus that is necessary for successful day trading results:

The Successful Day Trader's Focus

Well analyzed and —> Automatic execution —> Successful day
  strategized trade   (based on highly   trade results
  (based on   concentrated focus   (whether the
  probability)   and confidence)   trade makes a
                                                                        profit or loss)

State of Mind Management

To be successful at day trading you must constantly trade from a state of mind that allows you to maintain a high level of self-esteem, unshakable confidence, and laser straight focus. This state of mind is characterized by relaxation, focus without anxiety, self-trust, and resourcefulness.

The Successful Day Trader's State of Mind

Positive state —> Allows for unhesitating —> Positive trading
  of mind   implementation of   result
                              one's trading strategy

A positive state of mind is the result of consistently processing positive verbal attitudes, beliefs, and images that will enhance one's trading performance. The following are guides to positive processing:

- Expect the best of yourself.
- Establish a personal standard of excellence.
- Create an internal atmosphere for success based on visual, auditory, and feeling (kinesthetic) imagery that enhances performance.
- Communicate positively and effectively . . . with yourself! See yourself as positive, resourceful, and self-empowering.

- Rehearse a system of personal beliefs that can enhance your state of mind immediately.

The psychological skills that are necessary to day trade successfully require ongoing commitment and conditioning. They must be practiced day in, day out. I have been keeping up-to-date charts by hand in over 20 different commodities for more than 25 years. Technical analysis is very important. It is not, however, in my opinion, as important as working through the psychological and attitudinal issues of trading in general and day trading in particular.

The Syntax of Successful Day Trading

Well-analyzed trade

+

System of empowering personal beliefs
and attitudes

+

Proper execution based on positive focus

+

Decisive, resourceful state of mind

+

Successful trading performance

In his book *Melamed on the Markets* (Wiley, 1994), the legendary trader Leo Melamed observed:

> You learn to distinguish the good traders from the bad, the successful techniques from the unsuccessful, and the good habits from the faulty. You also learn to distinguish the lover from the fighter, the winners from the losers, the serious from the frivolous, the cerebral from the superficial, and the friend from the foe. But above all, you learn that the psychological makeup of the trader is the single most critical element of success.

The Essential Psychological Barriers to Successful Day Trading

What follows is a discussion of the essential barriers that inhibit or prevent traders from securing a positive market result. These barriers are:

- Not defining a loss
- Not taking a loss or profit
- Getting locked into a belief
- Trading on inside information or taking a tip
- Kamikaze trading
- Euphoric trading
- Hesitating at your numbers
- Not catching a breakout
- Not focusing on opportunities
- Being more invested in being right than in making money
- Trying to be perfect
- Not consistently applying your trading system
- Not having a well-defined money management system
- Not being in the right state of mind

Not defining a loss.   No one enters a trade expecting to lose! No one buys thinking the market will break, and, conversely, no one sells on the assumption that the market is about to rally to new highs . . . but to paraphrase a famous saying, things happen! It is essential for the day trader to identify without qualification his loss point before—not after—entering the trade. When you get stopped out, "just pick yourself up, dust yourself off, and start all over again."

According to Tony Saliba, market wizard:

Look both ways before you cross the street! I've heard it a million times, but you know what? A car almost hit me the other day. I was walking across Franklin, talking on the telephone with a trader upstairs, and I didn't notice that the light changed. A car just came down off the ramp, honked his horn and missed me by about two feet. It scared the hell out of me! My little four-year-old nephew said, "Uncle Tony, stop, look, and listen. Right?" It's a cliche! How many traders follow that market truth?

Not catching a loss or a profit.   Each day trade should have its own internal logic based on probability and consistent with your own methodology. When the market has moved to your exit point either on the upside or downside, you must react automatically without hesitation. That is to say, you must take the profit or loss. If the market continues to move in your direction once again, based on probability consistent with your technical bias, find a new entry point. Reentry is an essential element in any trading system. The point is that when the market does give you a profit, I believe it is essential that you take it. It is psychologically important that you walk away from the trade with change in your pocket!

Getting locked into a belief.   It's so easy to get locked into a jail cell of personal opinion. The market doesn't lie; it reveals all to the keen observer. You must not confuse your subjective opinion with the objective action of the market. Remember, the market feels no obligation to gratify your opinion! Day traders need to focus on a single rigorous method that works; all else is just another opinion. Money talks, all else walks!

Trading on inside information or taking a tip.   For losers only! By the time you've heard it, it has circulated widely. If you don't enjoy playing the role of salami entering the slicer, don't day trade on someone else's tip. Typically, this information comes from the phone men or trading desks. They will tell you that if the market gets below a certain level, the trader will start buying or selling. If they were so smart they'd be in the ring carding trades, not manning the phones!

Kamikaze trading. What more can I say! Crashing airplanes don't fly! If you feel angry, betrayed, in need of revenge . . . apply to law school! Don't trade, you'll crash land!

Euphoric trading. Euphoric trading is the opposite of Kamikaze trading. You're feeling invincible, heroic, bulletproof. You feel the lottery can't help but draw your ticket. As soon as you lose your objectivity, bullets start piercing flesh!

Hesitating at your numbers. Day traders don't have the luxury of hesitating once they have identified a setup trade. It is both financially and psychologically debilitating not to pick up the ball and run. The discipline always must be to take the trades that are consistent with your methodology no matter what! If you take the trade and get stopped out . . . welcome to the world of day trading. Remember, you can't score touchdowns without the ball.

Not catching a breakout. Another form of hesitation. It's like going to the airport and watching the planes take off. Wouldn't it be fun just once to get on board and arrive at an exciting destination?

Not focusing on opportunities. There are many (constant and consistent) distractions in the market. So much of day trading is just having the ability to get beyond the noise, the talk, and the smoke! Consistency in your approach with a high degree of confidence and optimism will keep your focus clear. You must find a way to get beyond all the head fakes!

Being more invested in being right than in making money. Is it your goal to be an analyst or a trader? You must know the answer to that question. If your technical analysis is turning you into a Ph.D. in a particular stock or market sector, join a university faculty; you'll save money! Trading is not about scholarship. It's about making money. That's not to say money should be the object of all efforts; I believe it shouldn't. But this is one game where the scorecard is denominated in hard currency. It's not enough to point to the fact that you had the high or low of the market!

In *The Disciplined Trader,* Mark Douglas wrote:

> I know it may sound strange to many readers, but there is an inverse relationship between analysis and trading results. More analysis or the ability to make more and finer distinctions in the market's behavior will not produce better trading results. Many traders find themselves caught in this exasperating loop, thinking that more or better analysis is going to give them the confidence they need to do what needs to be done to achieve success. I call this loop a trading paradox that most traders find it difficult, if not impossible, to reconcile until they realize you can't use analysis to overcome your fear of being wrong or losing money. It just doesn't work!

Trying to be perfect. You don't have to be perfect; merely excellent! Excellence produces results, perfection produces ulcers!

Not consistently applying your trading system. It is there for one purpose only . . . to be used so you can garner profits, letting them pile up like pleasing snow drifts!

Not having a well-defined money management system. There are literally hundreds of books written on this subject . . . You don't have to read them! For day trading purposes your trade should give you a minimum of a 2:1 risk-to-reward ratio.

Not being in the right state of mind. Funny, but it comes back down to this. In my experience, more than 90 percent of all trading failure is the result of not being in the right state of mind. The right state of mind produces the right results!

In our book *The Innergame of Trading,* my partner, Bob Koppel, and I wrote:

> It is our belief that continually elevating your state of mind by focusing on internal and external phenomena that allow you to stay resourceful and true to your trading strategy is the answer. We have demonstrated how to do this through processing positive beliefs and thoughts and by directing your physiology. When a negative thought comes into consciousness and begins to distract your focus, don't fight it. Acknowledge its existence and go forward.

Successful trading, in essence, comes down to this: Formulate a day trading plan that works, overcome your own personal psychological barriers, and condition yourself to produce feelings of self-trust, high self-esteem, and unshakable conviction and confidence. Doing this naturally leads to good judgment and winning trades with a proven methodology based on probability.

So what then is the edge that makes the difference in day trading? Let me suggest the following:

1. Fully understand your motives for trading. Once you know what your motives are, examine them carefully. Most traders trade in a constant state of conflict. From experience I've found that many people who think they want to day trade really don't.

2. Develop a personal strategy that works for you and fits your personality. If the system doesn't feel right, you're going to lose before you even start. Remember, by the very nature of day trading you must trade a system that is totally within your control.

3. It has to be fun. I can't stress this point enough. Trading has to literally feel good. You must be in a frame of mind that allows you to enjoy the process effortlessly, be resourceful, and make good judgments. Even when you are losing! You don't have to like it, but you do have to have a sense of humor.

4. Hard work is essential. There's no way to get around it. You must put in the time. As Thomas Edison said, "The reason a lot of people do not recognize opportunity is because it usually goes around wearing overalls, looking like hard work."

5. You must have confidence. You must possess a repertoire of personal beliefs that constantly reinforces feelings of high self-esteem and confidence in your analysis and execution of trades whether you win or lose. Needless to say, discipline, patience, personal responsibility, and repeated success in day trading make this a lot easier.

6. You need a positive state of mind. All top-performing traders have developed an internal terrain that reduces anxiety and promotes excellence. They manage to achieve this end by representing external events internally in such a way that ensures success, adjusting and redefining as they deem appropriate. They employ a belief system that doesn't allow for the concept of failure, and they adopt a personal focus that concentrates on what is essential to achieving this end. In short, they have mastered the ability to create states of mind and body that are resourceful and assure whatever it takes to succeed.

As another legendary trader, Jeffrey Silverman, observed when I interviewed him:

You must spend the time—you must study the characteristics of successful traders. You must study your own mistakes. You must study the mistakes of the others around you. Increasing levels of sophistication will put you in the direction of understanding who you are. You must really study your own self and understand what you're all about. It's not clear to me whether I didn't do this whole thing backwards where I studied the economics and science of trading and worked into the psychology of trading and finally got involved in some sort of philosophical thinking of the whole trading process. It's not clear to me that I didn't do the whole thing backward and shouldn't have studied philosophy and psychology at the start and it might have made the whole process easier.

Strategy and the Overall Game Plan

"All men can see those tactics whereby I conquer,
but what none can see is the strategy out of which
victory is evolved."
— *Sun-Tzu (fourth century B.C.)*

As a day trader it is important for you to be able to distinguish between trading strategy and trading tactics.

Trading strategy is the process of determining your major trading goals and then adopting a course of action whereby you allocate the resources necessary to achieve those ends. Trading tactics is the process of translating broad strategic goals into specific objectives that are relevant to a single component of your trading plan.

In Part Two when I discuss my own personal day trading system, The Digital Day Trading Method of Short-Term Trading, my focus is specific tactics and technical analytical considerations; however, to lay a framework for the strategic context of my system's application, I concentrate here on what I believe are the essential elements of a successful day trading strategy that underlie all tactical applications.

The Essential Elements of a Successful Day Trading Strategy

A successful strategy for day trading does the following:

- Assumes personal responsibility for all market actions
- Takes into consideration your motivation for trading
- Allows you to trade to win
- Establishes a clear, precise plan of action
- Creates a point of focus
- Is automatic and effortless in its implementation
- Manages risk and assumes losses
- Allows for patience
- Is practical and profit oriented
- Allows you to produce consistent results

Let's examine each of these characteristics of successful day trading more fully.

Assumes personal responsibility for all market actions. Traders often say they "make a profit" but "take a loss." The reality, of course, is that we do both. You the trader produce the results. This may seem obvious, but I can assure you, based on my 25 years of experience and having worked with hundreds of traders, it is the rare trader who truly lives by this credo! It isn't your broker, your brother-in-law, the chairman of the board of the Fed, the fill, the computer, the unemployment report—it's you! It's a simple fact that must be understood in the adoption of any trading strategy: You are responsible for the results. Good or bad, the buck stops (and starts) here!

Takes into consideration your motivation for trading. It is essential that your day trading approach takes into consideration your motive and motivation for trading. In addition, it is imperative that your method feels "right," which is to say it is consistent and congruent with your personality. If it doesn't feel natural, it is like taking a ten-mile hike in boots that are two sizes too small. Ask yourself exactly why you want to day trade? Are your personality and approach suitable?

Establishes a clear, precise plan of action. The recipe for success in trading is a simple one. Your plan of action needs only three elements:

1. It identifies a signal (opportunity).
2. It allows you to take immediate action (buy or sell).
3. It allows you to feel good no matter the result as long as the trade is consistent with your specific method or technical bias and was based on probability.

Most day traders, however, experience doubt or hesitate just at the moment of action. The way to overcome this is to have a crystal clear point of focus, which allows you to resolve the omnipresent internal and external hindrances.

Creates a point of focus. Staying fixed on your particular approach, method, or system is what will allow you to resolve all the debilitating emotions you experience while day trading. It is disciplining yourself to refocus back to your particular method, numbers, system, and the like that helps you to resolve your natural feelings of anxiety as you are experiencing them. I talk more about this later when I discuss the application of the Digital Day Trading Method. But for now the essential point is that you must know what you are looking for and what you are looking at in the market. You must be able to distinguish the signal from the noise and distinguish high probability from low probability trades.

Is automatic and effortless in its implementation.
The way all the hard work you have done as a trader pays off, in my opinion, is by allowing you to act absolutely, automatically, and effortlessly in the market when you have a high probability signal. The discipline is to "hard wire" your neurological system to act at just these times. By being in a position to "catch" those trades, you'll find your need to tell colleagues about the great trades that got away has been neutralized!

Manages risk and assumes losses.
The one constant shared by all traders is that they take losses. You can't be afraid to lose. Truly, I love the market to take me out and hit my day trading stops. I challenge it to do no less. Do I like to lose? Hell, no! But if the market takes me out, I have paid for some very valuable information. Of course, it goes without saying that my losses are always circumscribed.

Allows for patience.
Following your signal religiously teaches you to have patience rather than getting caught up in the minute-by-minute emotions of day trading. The key to success here is to give yourself the distance to make decisions that are based on a thoughtful process, method, and strategy rather than on the exciting emotional gyrations of the market.

According to Mark Douglas, author of *The Disciplined Trader:*

> There are certain characteristics of a mind-set that I believe are essential to creating success in the markets or creating consistency. To me, success as a trader is consistency. There is an often-used saying on the floor of the exchanges that "traders just rent their winnings." As you know, there are many traders who have reached the stage of development where they can put together a substantial string of winning trades for days, weeks, or even months, only to lose all or almost all of their

hard-won equity in a few trades and then start the process all over again. If a trader hasn't neutralized his susceptibility to giving his winnings back to the market, then he is not what I define as a successful trader.

Is practical and profit oriented. Many day traders get bogged down in the theoretical accuracy of their particular system. This is not necessarily important. What *is* important is performance. Making money supersedes theoretical attachment to a particular ideological or technical bias. I believe Winston Churchill said it best: "It is a socialist idea that making profits is a vice; I consider the real vice is making losses."

Allows you to produce consistent results. Although in trading you can never really have certainty, paradoxically, to operate effectively you must act with certainty—that is, resolutely at the point of decision. Consistency in day trading derives from applying a proven method without fail every time a signal is generated. Your trading system provides the organization that allows you to identify and exploit opportunities for achieving consistent results. It goes without saying, the rest is up to you! As Anthony Robbins has written in *Personal Power,* "The difference between those who succeed and those who fail isn't what they have—it's what they choose to see and do with their resources and their experiences of life."

Accordingly, your trading strategy should allow you to open your eyes and see market opportunities . . . so that you can act!

PART TWO

Trading on a Level Playing Field

4

Competing with the Market Makers

This chapter presents the essential elements of what you need to know for electronic intraday trading for small price increments. On exchange floors throughout the world this is called "scalping," and it is the provenance of traders who stand in trading pits and buy and sell throughout the day for their own accounts and those of clients. This same opportunity is now open to you.

The securities markets as they exist today are composed of two distinct systems: the specialist system and the market maker system.

The Specialist System

Traders on the New York Stock Exchange (NYSE) and the American Stock Exchange (AMEX) use a specialist system; that is, each stock traded on the exchange is assigned to a specialist who is expected to maintain an orderly market and keep a book of resting orders above and below the current market. The specialist not only bids and offers for others but also steps in during volatile price movements and uses his own capital to take the opposite side of either an excess of bids or offers. Of course, the price at which this occurs is determined by the supply and demand of the stock at that moment. For example, if a favorable earnings report is released for XYZ and there is an influx of buy orders, the specialist will use a combination of sell orders from the public, the book of resting orders, and his own capital to accommodate all the buy orders for XYZ. The price of XYZ will be determined by the sell orders available and, when those are exhausted, the experience and judgment of the specialist. You may have either seen or experienced a stock that opens several points above its previous day's close. This is the specialist attempting to find an appropriate price level.

The Market Maker System

The Nasdaq and over-the-counter (OTC) markets are traded through an electronic network, which brings together market makers, brokerage houses, and traders like you. This system gives everyone the opportunity to "see" the market by its display of bids and offers and the size of those bids and offers.

Currently there are three levels of available service:

1. The first is called *Level I* and provides real-time quotes that reflect the best bid and offer and their sizes. Brokerage houses and the majority of investors who are looking for the most recent quotes use this level of service.
2. *Level II* differs from Level I in that it shows the best bid and offer not only by size but also by the depth of the market. Depth refers to the market that exists behind the best bid and offer. It may show two or three other bids or offers at the best price and then will show the next best bid or offer for several levels up and down from the last price.
3. *Level III* has all the features of Level II and is used by market makers. It allows the market maker to constantly update the quotes for the securities they trade.

The Level II trading screen is your window to the world of the securities markets. It gives you real-time information such as stock quotes, bids, offers, volume, time of sales, and much more. Learning what information is available and when and how to use that information is key to beginning the process to successful digital day trading.

There are several software companies that produce the Level II information. For purposes of illustration in this book, we are using information from Tradecast, Inc. Also, we have included excerpts from the trader's manual in Appendix B for your reference with detailed descriptions and instructions.

Customized Windows in Level II Trading Software

Customized windows on your screen include:

- Blotter window
- Stock window

- Ticker window
- Time of sales window
- Board views windows
- Top ten windows
- Fundamental data window
- Order entry window

The blotter window. The blotter window comprises three panes: an open positions pane, a summary pane, and a trades pane. The open positions pane, shown in Figure 4.1, keeps track of your current open positions and is customizable with 25 different pieces of information that you may display in the format that suits you. A summary pane, as shown in Figure 4.2, contains information about the current day's trading, which can include equity, margin, P/L, number of trades, and realized and unrealized profit and loss. The trades pane, in Figure 4.3,

FIGURE 4.1 The Open Positions Pane

Blotter: CMOORE						
Open Positions		Summary		Trades		
Symbol	Side	Shares	Cost		P/L	Trade Time
EBAY	B	1000	160.50	22,562.50		14:43:00
INTC	B	1000	114.56	1,625.00		11:49:00
WCOM	B	1000	60.94	812.50		11:57:00

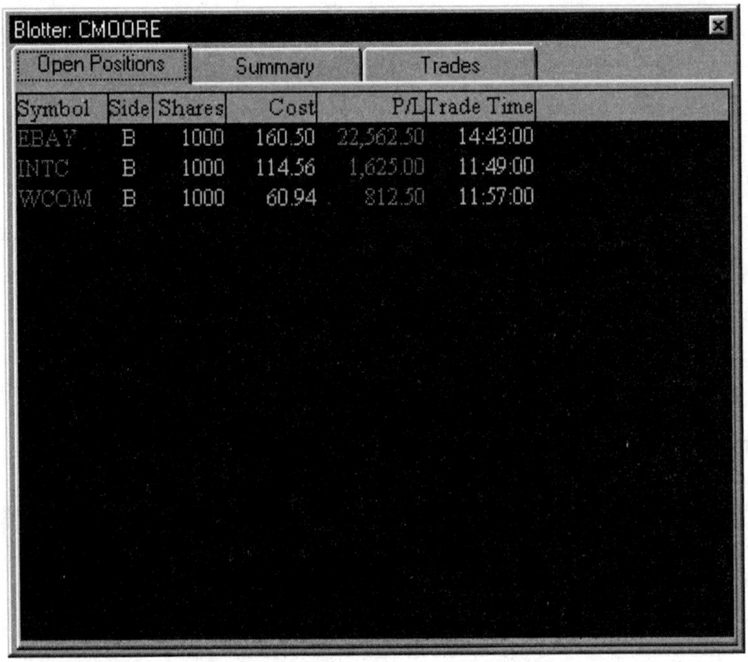

FIGURE 4.2   The Summary Pane

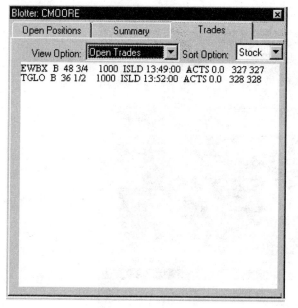

```
Blotter: CMOORE                                    [x]
┌─────────────┬──────────────┬─────────────┐
│Open Positions│  Summary     │  Trades     │
│ Trades Today:              8              He│
│ Current Margin:   1,914,750.00            │
│ ┌ Profit and Loss ──────────────┐    Sym...│
│ │ Realized            1,062.50   │         │
│ │ Unrealized          6,125.00   │         │
│ ┌ Exposure ─────────────────────┐         │
│ │ Long               85,250.00   │         │
│ │ Short                   0.00   │         │
│ │ Current            85,250.00   │         │
│ ┌ Open ─────────────────────────┐         │
│ │ Positions               2      │         │
│ │ Trades                  2      │         │
│ ┌ Equity ───────────────────────┐         │
│ │ Startup           100,000.00   │         │
│ │ Current         1,000,000.00   │         │
│ ┌ Shares ───────────────────────┐         │
│ │ Long                2,000      │         │
│ │ Short                   0      │         │
│ │ Total               2,000      │         │
└─────────────────────────────────┘         │
```

FIGURE 4.3   The Trades Pane

```
Blotter: CMOORE                                    [x]
┌─────────────┬──────────────┬─────────────┐
│Open Positions│  Summary     │  Trades     │
│ View Option: [Open Trades ▼] Sort Option: [Stock ▼]│
│ EWBX B 48 3/4  1000 ISLD 13:49:00 ACTS 0.0  327 327│
│ TGLO B 36 1/2  1000 ISLD 13:52:00 ACTS 0.0  328 328│
│                                           │
└───────────────────────────────────────────┘
```

allows you to view all trades, today's trades, open trades short positions, long positions, and completed trades.

The stock window. The stock window, in Figure 4.4, is an all-purpose window that supplies most of the information available from Level I and Level II. This information includes individual stock symbols, quotes, bids and offers, various ECNs, and market maker information. This window also can be customized and usually serves as the centerpiece of your trading screen.

The ticker window. The ticker window, shown in Figure 4.5, will keep you updated on price changes in several different combinations. The position ticker will display changes to those stocks that you hold as open positions. A long ticker will display only those stocks that you are currently long. You also have the ability to add any stock you wish to follow merely by clicking on its symbol in the stock window and dragging it to the ticker window. The ticker gives you a continuous update of any number of stocks you may be currently interested in.

FIGURE 4.4   The Stock Window

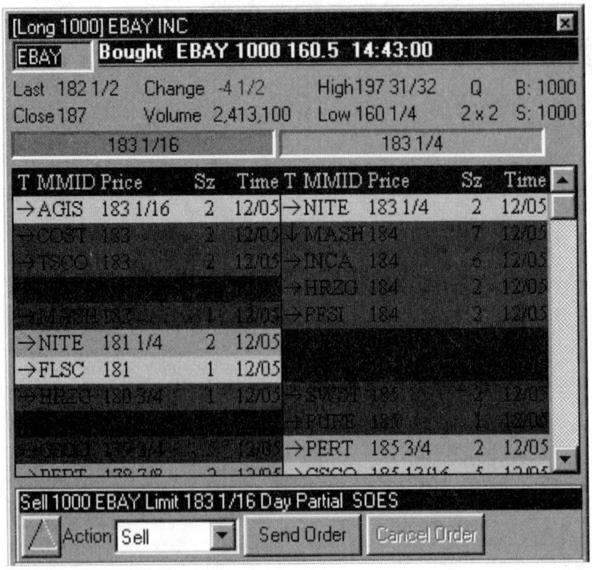

FIGURE 4.5   The Ticker Window

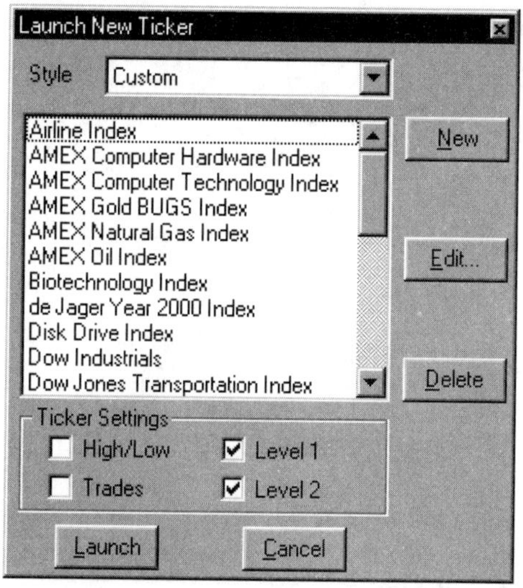

Time of sales window.   This window displays the actual time of the sale of a stock, its bid or offer, and the number of shares traded. Some traders use this window to get a good idea of price sequence. (See Figure 4.6.)

Board views windows.   The board view, shown in Figure 4.7, is similar to the blotter and will list as many symbols as you like, along with information such as bid, offer, high, low, close, last size, time, change, and volume. You may customize several board windows if you wish.

Top ten windows.   Top ten windows, shown in Figure 4.8, give you the opportunity to monitor the big winners and losers during the trading day. The categories are for each individual exchange or market and include:

- Gainers/Losers
- Percentage gainers/losers
- Volume

FIGURE 4.6   Time of Sales Window

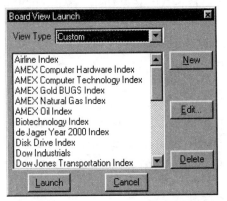

```
INTC                            ☒
┌─────────────────────┐
│                     │
└─────────────────────┘
14:27     101 1/16      200 Q   ▲
14:27     101 1/8       400 Q
14:27     101 1/8       500 Q
14:27 a   101 1/8        30 Q
14:27 b   101 1/16        5 Q
14:27 a   101 1/8        30 Q
14:27 b   101 1/16       10 Q
14:27     101 1/8       300 Q
14:27 a   101 1/8        30 Q U
14:27 b   101 1/16       10 Q U
14:27     101 1/16      100 Q
14:27     101 1/16      100 Q
14:27 a   101 1/8        30 Q
14:27 b   101            10 Q
14:27     101         30000 Q
14:27     101 1/16     3500 Q
14:26     101 3/32     1000 Q
14:26 a   101 1/16       30 Q
14:26 b   101            10 Q
14:26     101 1/16      200 Q
14:26     100 5/16      200 Q X  ▼
```

FIGURE 4.7   Board Views

```
Board View Launch                          ☒

View Type  [Custom            ▼]

┌────────────────────────────────┐   ┌─────────┐
│Airline Index                 ▲ │   │  New    │
│AMEX Computer Hardware Index    │   └─────────┘
│AMEX Computer Technology Index  │
│AMEX Gold BUGS Index            │
│AMEX Natural Gas Index          │   ┌─────────┐
│AMEX Oil Index                  │   │  Edit... │
│Biotechnology Index             │   └─────────┘
│de Jager Year 2000 Index        │
│Disk Drive Index                │
│Dow Industrials                 │   ┌─────────┐
│Dow Jones Transportation Index▼ │   │ Delete  │
└────────────────────────────────┘   └─────────┘

     [  Launch  ]        [  Cancel  ]
```

Symbol	Bid	Ask	Close	Open	Last	Size	Time	Change	High	Low	Volume
APM	7 1/16	7 1/8	7 1/2	7 3/8	7 1/16	200	11:20	-0 7/16	7 3/8	7 1/16	89,500
HMTT	12 9/16	12 5/8	12 1/2	12 1/2	12 5/8	200	11:19	0 1/8	12 7/8	12 1/2	15,900
HTCH	32 5/8	33	32	31 3/4	33	1,300	11:18	1	33 1/4	31 3/4	177,600
IOM	8	8 1/16	7 13/16	7 15/16	8	500	11:20	0 3/16	8 1/8	7 7/8	1,337,100
KMAG	10 13/16	10 15/16	10 15/16	11	10 7/8	500	11:20	-0 1/16	11 1/4	10 7/8	223,900
QNTM	20 7/8	20 15/16	21 5/8	21 7/8	20 7/8	1,000	11:20	-0 3/4	22	20 7/8	800,900
RDRT	16 9/16	16 5/8	16 15/16	16 7/8	16 9/16	100	11:20	-0 3/8	16 7/8	16 1/2	196,600
SEG	31 13/16	31 15/16	32 3/8	32 11/16	31 15/16	1,000	11:20	-0 7/16	32 11/16	31 7/8	523,300
STK	33 1/8	33 3/16	33	33 7/8	33 1/8	2,300	11:20	0 1/8	34	32 3/4	218,000
WDC	15 1/2	15 9/16	15 3/4	15 7/8	15 9/16	500	11:20	-0 3/16	16	15 7/16	313,100

Board View [Disk Drive Index]

FIGURE 4.8   Top Ten

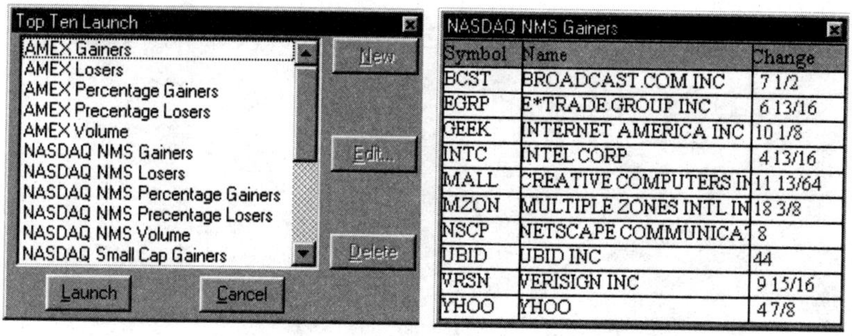

- Nasdaq small cap gainers/losers
- Nasdaq small cap percentage gainers/losers
- Nasdaq national Market System Composite (NMS) gainers/losers
- Nasdaq NMS percentage gainers/losers
- Nasdaq NMS volume

Fundamental data window.   This window displays fundamental information that is not displayed on any other windows (see Figure 4.9). Some of the information includes:

- Rank
- Beta
- Price-earnings ratio
- 52-week high/low
- Year high/low
- Average daily volume
- Dividend rate
- Earnings
- Earnings comment
- Financial comment
- Earnings estimates

FIGURE 4.9   Fundamental Data Window

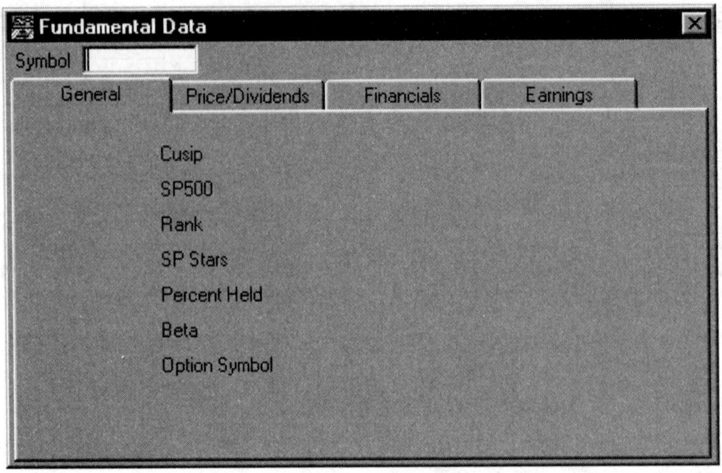

Order entry window.   This window lets you see the status of your pending orders. (See Figure 4.10.) The window also displays a list of executions and message logs.

The overview of the Level II capability shown here is merely an introduction to the information that is available to the trader. The flexibility of the windows and the various ways to manipulate the information make this a powerful tool. This information and technology will allow you to enter and exit markets, gather the latest information, and keep tabs on hundreds of stocks—all of which puts you on equal footing with professional traders.

The first consideration for the beginning day trader is to familiarize himself or herself with the use of the Level II screens. It is important to learn the information that they convey and how to use that information. Next, practice the physical aspects of order entry and exit to take advantage of the edge that the system gives to you.

As you read and analyze the ideas and information in the interviews that follow, you will begin to see and understand how you can compete on an equal playing field with professional market makers.

FIGURE 4.10 Order Entry Windows

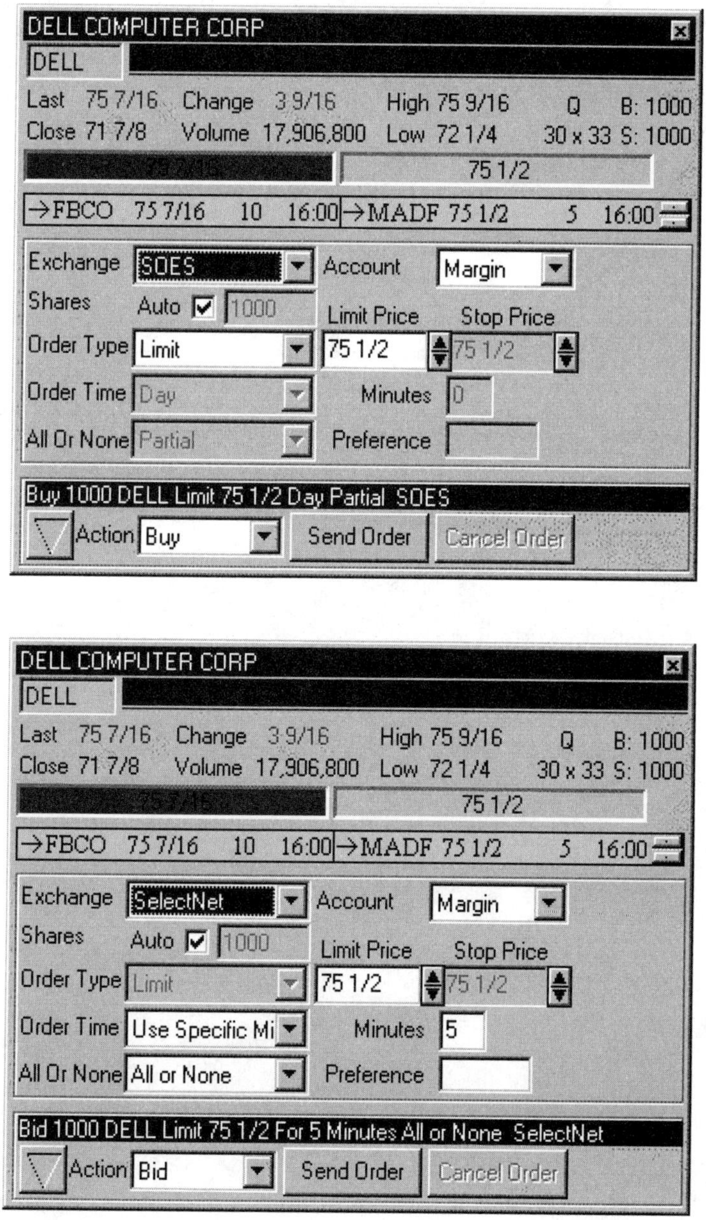

5

David Jamail

David Jamail is a professional day trader and a principal in Cornerstone Securities.

Q: David, what first attracted you to electronic day trading?

DAVID: As you know, I've been a trader for a long time. To answer your question specifically: I wanted to be able to scalp the market without having to be in Chicago or New York.

Q: You mean, like being in the pit?

DAVID: It's the closest thing to being there without really being there.

Q: What kind of trading did you do before you got involved with digital day trading?

DAVID: I traded listed stocks for my own account. In the 1980s I was a broker at E.F. Hutton and PaineWebber.

Q: So you have experience trading the old-fashioned way?

DAVID: Exactly. Calling down to the floor and putting in orders—a far cry from what I do now!

Q: What exactly brought you to this arena of trading on an electronic platform?

DAVID: In 1993 I was a partner in a brokerage firm in Houston, and two guys I know brought SOES terminals into our office. After watching them trade SOES for about a month, I realized its obvious benefits: direct access to the market and the ability to trade with virtually no slippage. Day trading like this was very attractive to me, and I gave up the other type of trading.

Q: Can you describe what specific actions you take on a daily basis to prepare yourself for the trading day?

DAVID: I scan all the news sources, Bloomberg, and Reuters for headlines and for analyst upgrades and downgrades. I also look at earnings reports and any other news that may affect the mid-cap or large-cap stocks. Then I look through the 300 charts of the universe of stocks that I normally trade, searching for particular setups and chart patterns.

Q: Would you say you're primarily a chart pattern trader?

DAVID: My primary input is charts. Initially, I work off a daily chart and then key off a two-minute intraday chart.

Q: How would you contrast electronic trading from conventional trading?

DAVID: Well, for one thing, there's so much less overhead involved in executing the trade. You're freer to make more trades than you would normally be able to do using a broker. I'm more prolific as a trader. I don't know that there is much difference in what I do fundamentally, except that before I couldn't physically call out all the orders, execute them, and have them reported back to me in the volume I day trade today.

Q: What specific stocks do you trade, and how do arrive at your portfolio mix?

DAVID: Basically, we scan all 5,000 Nasdaq stocks. We watch the ticker for new highs and lows. Every time that a new high or low appears, my partner and I pull up the stock to see if it has the kind of pattern that warrants a buy or sell signal. Typically, we're breakout traders. Ninety-five percent of all my trades are buys at new highs or sells at new lows to initiate the position.

Q: Do you usually trade for a single day or a couple of days?

DAVID: Our primary exit method, which applies to the majority of our trades, uses a trailing stop somewhere between $\frac{3}{4}$ point and $1\frac{1}{4}$ point for a big-cap stock. Internet stocks are more volatile. For them, we'll use a 3-, 4-, or 5-point trailing stop loss, depending on the spread and market volatility.

Q: How did you arrive at this day trading method?

DAVID: It evolved as a result of observing the market action indicated in intraday charts; for example, analyzing in a five-day period what are the deepest retracements after a breakout. Let's say a stock has an average range of $3\frac{1}{2}$ points with an average pullback of $\frac{3}{4}$ to 1 point. We looked at those kind of stocks and tried to buy them on a retracement after a new high and, over time, just tried to buy as many of those patterns as we could. Of course, we also would cull out the losers as they broke down beyond our defined parameters.

Q: How do you handle the winners?

DAVID: As I said, we hold them until they pull back at least 1 point after a new high. It may take one, two, or three days for that to happen.

Q: Do you find that's also true for the short side of the market after you've taken a sell signal?

DAVID: No. The short moves have been quicker, so you don't really stay in them as long. We probably are in as many as 150 names at a time. But we're also turning our portfolio over three or four times a day. I mean, some stocks we're in and out of within an hour.

Q: Because they back off?

DAVID: Right. We buy them and the trend reverses. And then an hour later, it runs up 3 points, and we start the process all over again.

Q: With 150 names, how do you keep track of all your trades?

DAVID: Through our software we're tracking tickers of all the Nasdaq Level II data of all the stocks that we're in. Every time we buy or sell a stock to initiate a position, it puts it in a ticker so we see all Level I and Level II data on that stock. Also, I have an assistant who only tracks new highs and new lows.

Q: Do you put an actual stop in the market or just wait for the dollar pullback?

DAVID: We wait for the dollar pullback, because you can't put a physical sell stop in the market for a Nasdaq stock. Most days we don't trade any New York stock, just because we don't get the same level of information. It's harder to get a feel for New York over the DOT system, so in general we focus on the Nasdaq.

Q: What unique considerations do you feel distinguish day trading from a longer-term approach?

DAVID: Typically, I think you can better calculate and control your risk. I believe the risk-reward ratio is better in day trading. I mean, looking at all the traders around us, an average gaining day seems much better than the buy-and-hold, risk-adjusted approach.

Many of the trades we make just wouldn't make sense for a longer term. We're looking for much shorter-term moves where we think we can observe momentum building. It's just the unique aspect of the Level II trade of the market makers. In general, it's more the market maker's impetus for doing a lot of trades rather than the chart pattern or earnings expectations of a particular stock.

Q: On what time frame charts do you generally concentrate?

DAVID: Normally, I look at two charts; that is, every time I pull up a stock it automatically pulls up two charts. One of them is the past 150 days, daily candlestick, high, low, open, close for the day. Also, I look at the same high, low, open, close data for the previous two days on a two-minute interval—that is, two days' worth of tick data on a two-minute candlestick chart. And that helps me get a sense of where the shorter-term support and resistance come in.

Q: How do you manage the risk overall?

DAVID: We're very disciplined and diligent about that. The way we control risk is as follows: No matter what we think about a stock, if the pattern is violated (by definition, any stock that's 2 points off the high), we punch a button and whack the bid and get out of the stock! I mean, the one thing we don't hesitate to do is get out of losers. For us there's no pain associated with selling a stock that's down. I see a lot of day traders or traders, especially when they start, think that if they're losing money in a stock they need to make it back in the same stock. They buy the stock, it's down a point from when they bought it, and they've got a resistance to sell it out! They go into a "hope" mode. And I think that's when risk really starts to creep in.

In day trading or trading in general, you really need to have a disciplined strategy where risks are not greater than rewards. The risk-reward ratio must make sense. The first thing too many traders want to do is ring the cash register. They buy a stock, it goes up ½ point, then it down ticks. They might be in three stocks. They want to sell the stock that's up ½ point instead of the stock that's down ½ point. I don't know why . . . I mean, I do know. There's ego involved. They say to themselves, "Gosh, I bought a stock and it didn't work out!" They go into denial.

I'm a strong believer that making money comes from staying with the momentum. I have no problem selling stocks that have moved against me surrounded by stocks that are experiencing buying pressure.

Q: As you have said, David, many traders have difficulty doing that. Is that correct?

DAVID: Yes. A lot of traders experience a sort of psychological handicap. I mean, as they go through the normal learning curve, at first it's hard to read the market. They make mistakes; they push the wrong button. They do things that just don't make sense. But what is ultimately the most costly to their performance is frustration.

One of the first things new traders do is to get contractive— that is, to quickly take winners. If you don't do anything else that is different than learn to hold onto winners, I believe it will radically change your risk-reward profile. It distinguishes traders who barely make a living from the big traders. I've been a full-time electronic day trader since January 1993. For the first three and a half years, I was a pure scalper. If I saw a stock moving up, I would buy it, and the average trade was probably 45 to 90 seconds long. As soon as I bought it for ⅛, I was trying to sell it for ⅜.

Q: Was that successful?

DAVID: Yes, but I decided to change in 1996. A friend of mine came over in early 1996, and I saw him trade with expanded parameters and catch much greater market moves. He also would make the market prove him wrong. He would have 4-, 5-, 9-point winners at the same quantity of trades I was doing. Finally it dawned on me that I had to change my mindset. The riskiest thing about trading is *not* being in the market when it's going your way. Missing the upside is a whole lot more expensive over time than being in a little bit too long. I don't know if that has any meaning to you. It has dramatically transformed my profitability in the market. From making $500,000 to $800,000 a year to making over $4 million in 1998, and $1.8 million just last month. Basically, what has happened is that I've gained more confidence to make bigger bets and be in the market when it starts going my way. Also, I try to distill and analyze what's really different about what I'm doing versus the other trades I see around me. The risk of being out of the market when you must be in!

Q: David, what has been your most successful trade?

DAVID: That's a tough question considering how many stocks we trade. We're probably trading an average of 1,200 or 1,300 shares at a time. Sometimes I'll trade 5,000 shares of bigger, more liquid stocks. To answer your question: When the Internet stocks rolled over a couple of weeks ago, we sold Yahoo and Amazon and Excite short—just as they broke a big up trend line. We sold the stock and made 80 points in about four hours. They all went into a free fall after that. The point is: You have to be able to enter a trade and maintain your risk profile and have it work as well as that. That is what makes all the difference.

Q: And you were able to maintain your risk profile?

DAVID: Yes, we didn't have to take unusual risks to achieve that kind of performance.

Q: It was a one-way move, a no-brainer!

DAVID: Right. And the only way to screw it up is to get out too early. You also really have to focus on maintaining the right psychological state to trade in. The best defense is a good offense! I see a lot of traders burn out. They're always trading highly volatile stocks that jerk them in and jerk them out. You know, we trade for a living; we've got to be here five days a week. So there's a real advantage to pacing yourself psychologically. If you get in positions where you're sitting on the edge of your seat too much, you'll go into a hope mode. Eventually, you'll burn out and avoid trading. You'll enter fewer positions and start inventing reasons not to trade. A lot of our decisions are made as much on that basis: What's the real cost to us in terms of trader brain resources that are taken on a given trade versus how much can I make on this one stock?

Q: Well isn't psychology really the name of the game in short-term trading?

DAVID: It is, and I don't think it's that well defined to the average day trader. But if you sit down and really try to maximize what resources you have, the right psychological approach can greatly enhance your market results. We want to come in and try to take $100,000 a day out of the market. And you know, I'd rather do it with as little volatility as possible, because it's a lot easier to sift through the ups and downs that way. To me it's a lot easier to be in 100 positions and 100 names because I do get some diversification effect. And I get a spread effect, or whatever. And typically, I'm 80 percent and 90 percent on one side of the market. I mean, I'm not really that diversified. I want to do a bunch of different positions that kind of minimizes the negative effect of any one trade.

Q: Isn't your 100 names going to do what the overall market is doing on any particular day?

DAVID: Well, you know, I don't think that the correlation is as high as a lot of people think it is. I mean, with a lot of stocks, there's a significant disparity relative to the composite or Russell 2000. And so there's a lot of room to significantly outperform the averages every day by picking the right 100 stocks versus the 2,000 stocks in the Russell or the composites.

Q: David, how long did it take you to familiarize yourself with the electronic platform?

DAVID: Probably a good two to three months.

Q: So it really was important to spend time and focus on learning the platform?

DAVID: I think you can learn enough just to get started in a couple of days, a week or so in terms of what the buttons do. I'm assuming you know and understand what a bid and an offer are and what the different execution systems are—whether they're SOES or Selectnet or Island and how to interface them. I think you can learn how to punch the buttons in a week. To achieve "video game" reaction time, that is, to reach a professional level of efficiency, takes a couple of months.

Q: Now you're not trading for $\frac{1}{8}$ or $\frac{1}{4}$ or $\frac{1}{2}$, but you still feel it's necessary to get up to a reflex level of functioning on the platform.

DAVID: Yes, because I'm trying to manage 100 names at a time. You know, I'm doing 1,000 trades a day and probably buying or selling stock every 15 seconds on an average day. So, any enhanced efficiencies in terms of proficiency in monitoring and executing new positions pays real dividends.

Q: How has electronic trading changed your perception of the overall market?

DAVID: Differently at different times. More recently, probably in the past year and a half with the popularity of the ECNs, there are more public customers in the market as a percentage of trades. I've found the added liquidity has dampened some of the volatility in some of the moves—maybe $\frac{1}{8}$, maybe not as much. But certainly you don't have quite the swing when you have all these day traders. The whole mass psychology effect of trading, fear, and greed kind of tempers movement. I favor taking a little longer-term perspective, meaning longer than just the next ⅛ or ¼. You know, the stock goes up, and all of the people that bought it here are now offering it at the top. Then as soon as they get taken out, it goes up to the next level, they buy the stock at 115, and everybody is offering 115⅛. You see all the 115⅛ prints get taken. The next group of day traders are buying it from the other day traders who want to make ⅛, and it kind of stair-steps up and up. If it were just up to the Goldman Sachs and the First Bostons only representing the bids and the offers, they would be a little better at disguising what's going on. They're not nearly as transparent. And so I think it has been easier to read the market by watching the order flow of the ECMs and the day traders.

Q: David, you alluded to the idea that you're looking for particular patterns. Do you think that increased participation helps achieve the patterns that you're looking for?

DAVID: I think it does filter some of the "noise" out of the pattern where Goldman is a particularly effective market maker and he's got 300,000 to buy. For a period of time he can make it look like the stock is going down if other ECMs and participants weren't visible to the whole market, showing that there really are buyers out there. It's harder for the market makers to really disguise their intentions with all the new public customers in the market.

Q: Well, in the end I think it's probably is a good thing.

DAVID: I think it dampens volatility. And if it dampens volatility, that's good for investors and a fair price is represented more of the time than not, rather than just six market makers deciding what price they want to post at any one given time.

Q: What would be your advice to an aspiring digital day trader?

DAVID: I think the first thing is to assess why he or she wants to become a day trader. Honestly enjoying the process of trading or the "video game" skills required or the information-gathering process, rather than just viewing it as an easier way of making money, is an essential first step. Then, once the trader decides trading is consistent with his or her personality, he or she will need to commit for six and a half hours a day and think of it like graduate school. There's a cost to learning digital day trading, and you're going to lose money for three to six months, depending on the market conditions and how quickly you can learn the right psychological attitudes about taking losses and holding winners.

Once the trader accepts the analogy of going to graduate school, then he or she will have a great job after graduating. But don't expect to make any money, and you're going to have to pay the tuition! You must also learn how to calculate and manage risk. To know trading is not the same as rolling dice.

You need to have a plan and understand the risk reward of every strategy, tactic, and trade. Once you do start day trading, you will be using real money, trading 100 shares at a time to test market ideas. In my opinion, your only risk in the first three to six months of trading is running out of capital. And so, being out of the business is a big risk. Really, you need to understand that it may cost $20,000 or $30,000 to learn how to trade. Of course, nobody wants to lose that kind of money, but when you do, you must know it's not going to be the end of the world. Be fully prepared, psychologically strong, and knowledgeable about both the risks and rewards of day trading.

6

Stuart Shalowitz

Stuart Shalowitz is a professional day trader of stocks residing in Chicago.

Q: What first attracted you to electronic day trading?

STUART: I was introduced to day trading by a friend of mine from college. Basically, he told me that trading this way was the wave of the future. This was in early 1995. What attracted me was—and bear in mind I was no great floor trader and didn't have a lot of capital—just the sense that the future was going electronic, that people would be trading in cyberspace. Also, I knew a couple of traders who were making a very nice living day trading.

Q: Could you describe what specific actions you take on a daily basis to prepare for your trading?

STUART: I try to get in at least 45 minutes to one hour before the market opens. I have a daily routine: I read through *Investors*

63

Business Daily, The Wall Street Journal, the research that Cornerstone compiles, and various news reports. I also check out earnings and which stocks are hot. I'm also aware of where the market is opening and current futures prices to get a sense of the general market. I don't come in with a lot of set plays or preconceived notions of what the market is going to do, but I do want to know where the market is trading and what sectors are going to be hot. Also, I look at my account and make sure all my positions are in order. In truth, I really don't do any deep analytical stuff in terms of trading stocks.

Q: How would you contrast electronic trading with conventional trading?

STUART: The main difference with day trading electronically is the personal interaction with the market. You control your own orders, prices, volume, timing, and overall market action. There's so much creativity involved today in trading the Nasdaq, for instance. With my software, if I want to buy a stock, there are at least ten different ways I can enter the trade. You're not waiting for a broker; you're directly interacting with the market. With a Nasdaq stock, there is no floor or trading exchange; everything is cyberspace. And physical location is unimportant. You may have a market maker in a particular stock in Los Angeles who works for a firm out of New York. So to sum up, the big difference is the trader's direct interface with the market and the speed and control of execution. You know, the speed and power of the electronic trading platform are just mind boggling!

Q: You said a moment ago that you had different options for buying and selling stocks electronically, could you be more specific?

STUART: In terms of the Nasdaq system, you can buy a stock through the Small Order Execution System, or SOES, from a market maker only. That can be PaineWebber, Merrill-Lynch,

Morgan-Stanley, etc. If I don't want to use SOES, I can also go through any one of the eight ECNs (electronic communications networks).

Q: Which do you prefer?

STUART: In terms of day trading, Island, in my opinion, is probably the fastest and most widely used; however, I personally prefer SOES. It's not only more cost effective (only 50 cents per transaction rather than 1½ cents per share) but also entails trading with a market maker.

If the market is not really moving, I will invariably go SOES because it's cheaper. It saves me $14.50 (on 1,000 shares). Also, I know that if I hit a market maker, I can see what someone like PaineWebber did—refresh a bid or an offer, meaning replace the shares I bought or sold, or better yet, drop down a level. In other words, if I bought them at ¼, did PaineWebber go to ⅜ or ½? Did they flip over the bid? I want to know! Did I move them out of the way? Now, after they take that initial hit, they can refresh their bid to 100 or put up 2,000, whatever they want. It's all part of the game. They might have 20,000 to sell and just do 1,000 at a time. But, none of that bothers me; it's just additional information.

Q: Eventually, the market is going to do what it's going to do!

STUART: Yes, and I'm a firm believer in that. Although lately, the proliferation of day trading on the Nasdaq, I believe, has artificially run up stocks—in other words, increased the volatility.

Q: Run up stocks? Are you referring to the Internet stocks or the market in general?

STUART: Both. At times you will see stocks certainly rip up. And the sole reason is there is a finite number of people selling and a greater number of people buying, which sets up near-term volatility and allows for a good short-term sale.

Q: What specific stocks do you trade, and how do you arrive at the mix?

STUART: I tend to trade a lot of mid-cap Nasdaq stocks. I understand them and feel I know the way they move a little bit more. I don't trade the Dow or what people call the dirty dozen (Microsoft, Intel, Cisco, etc.) for a couple of reasons. I believe they are overly populated with traders and volume. I mean, they trade the 16th spread; that is to say, they tend to be very tightly traded stocks. Probably more importantly, the market makers in those stocks are some of the best market makers around. It can be Goldman-Sachs or some other pro—they're very good.

Q: And they have a lot of capital.

STUART: Unbelievable amounts of capital. They put on big positions. They're just very good traders, and they know how to work the stocks. Now if I'm going to sit and trade all day, I'd much rather trade against a younger guy who is a little wet behind the ears, just out of school, maybe trading some of the mid-cap stocks. He or she is a market maker whose system isn't as good as mine. And I feel I can work some of the mid-cap stocks and get in and out easily.

Q: What are the specific techniques that you work with and have found reliable over time?

STUART: I use a couple of different techniques. I'll trade off basic momentum, the direction in which the market is moving, focusing on the particular sectors that are moving and using a combination of technical indicators. I try to keep my approach pretty simple. The more simple, the better the result. I don't think stock trading is rocket science. I've done many more complicated things that frankly didn't work, which is to say that the trading part is not the most difficult thing. The simplicity is great because it allows me to focus on money management and psychology. So in general, if a stock is going up and I feel there's a lot of buying pressure coming in or it's bottoming out,

I will buy it. I watch the moving averages. I look at 20 and 50 days. In a strong market, you see everything hugging a 20-day moving average, finding support there. In a weaker market, I'll use a 50-day. So, it depends on the market.

Q: Specifically, how do you use the moving averages?

STUART: I'll buy the stock when it starts to spike up off the average. It might go sideways, it might come down and start to find support there. I'm not too big on catching falling knives, but when the market was beat up late last year, there were some stocks I did buy because I knew they were good companies. Stocks that traded literally at $60 or $70 were crushed to $5 and $6. Little stocks that are good companies. I didn't analyze PE ratios or dividends, just stocks that I felt had come back when the market turned.

Q: Do you use a tick chart?

STUART: Yes. I keep two candlestick charts on my machine. I have a daily chart that goes back from 135 to 150 days with the moving averages so I can track where the stock has been. I also use an intraday three-minute candlestick bar chart. I trade more off momentum than anything else.

Q: What do you mean by momentum?

STUART: I perceive the stock is bottoming and ticks up or simply observe that the market makers are piling on the bid. Really, it could be that simple!

Q: Piling on?

STUART: Maybe they're all starting to bid 30⅛ and I feel the stock is going up. I'll take a shot and buy it.

Q: And the advantage you have, again, is seeing the bids and the offers and how deep they go.

STUART: Exactly. You see the depth for the bid and the offer. As far as I'm concerned, buying the stock, that is, initiating the trade, is not the hard part. Anyone can tell you to buy Microsoft. It's the person who knows when to sell Microsoft, when to get out, that's the real test. So many times I can buy a stock thinking I'm only risking $\frac{1}{8}$. Or sometimes I'll buy stocks knowing I'll let the stock fold $\frac{1}{2}$ point against me or more. It just depends on the market and if I have profit in it. It sounds silly, but you know, that's the way it is! People ask me how much I let a stock go against me. The real answer is, it depends. It depends on the stock, it depends on the day, it depends on how much money I'm up or down in that stock. I'm never going to get it exactly perfect. A slew of things are constantly going through my head. Managing risk becomes a dynamic thing. It's not set in stone. Really, I think money management and risk management are the most important considerations for trading.

Q: When you're trading your entire portfolio of stocks, do you always know exactly how the entire portfolio is performing?

STUART: Not exactly. I pretty much microanalyze each trade. For example, I have certain stocks I won't let go against me even $\frac{1}{2}$ point, because I know if I'm wrong, I'm going to be really wrong and I don't want to deal with that! Whereas with other stocks, I'll give more of a back and fill.

Q: But your cardinal rule is, Never take a large loss?

STUART: Without doubt, always take small losses! I have a few little rules. I mean, I definitely try to be consistent and disciplined. If you're going to have small winners, you can't have big losers. You can make money having small winners. There are traders who do this every day and pound out a great deal of profit from the market. The key is that they manage their money. I mean, it's simple: If you have more winners than losers and your winners are bigger than your losers, you always will make money. I mean, you have to! That's just the way it is. We try to teach newer traders how to make a little money in order to help them mold a profitable style. For most people who day trade and want to go home flat, the goal is simply to leave the office with more money than they came with every single day. But again, money management and risk control are essential. Everyone is different. No two people have the same risk tolerance.

Q: How long did it take to familiarize yourself with the electronic platform?

STUART: The software keeps changing all the time. It can take people anywhere from a few days to weeks or even a month. The main thing to keep in mind is how powerful a tool this is. If you lift your finger off a button or incorrectly click a mouse, you're buying a lot of stock. And if you do that with a Microsoft or a Dow, you might never want to make that big a purchase in your life! So to answer your question, most of the software is user friendly but it's extremely powerful. In terms of time, depending on the person, from a few days to a few weeks. As you know, many firms have training programs or classes that teach the software.

Q: What advice do you have for an aspiring electronic day trader?

STUART: The first is that you want to look around. Find a firm where you feel comfortable, that is going to help you become a profitable trader. Second, understand this is definitely not a game. I mean, people come in and see the screens and the colors, and it looks exciting, but it is extremely competitive and highly intense. This is trading! There's a lot of money flying back and forth and you want to have good discipline and money management skills, as well as strong support from a firm that will help you progress as a trader. You can be successful, but it takes a lot of hard work.

7

Andy Kershner

*A*ndy Kershner *is a professional day trader of stocks and a principal of Cornerstone Securities.*

Q: What first attracted you to electronic day trading?

ANDY: A friend of mine figured out how to pick stocks; that is, he thought he could predict which ones were going to go up based on technical analysis. We put our money together, all of $5,000, and started trading options. As it turned out, a lot of our ideas were right, but the executions were poor, so we naturally gravitated toward electronic day trading. Electronic day trading allowed for better fills and information than we were receiving.

Q: When was this?

ANDY: The spring of 1994. For me, it started getting pretty heavy duty in July of 1995. Before that I did an average of only a couple trades a day. My trading was more long-term position trading.

Q: And then you made it more short term?

ANDY: Yes, because someone funded me, that is, funded a $100,000 account for me. From there, I started trading on a much grander scale and really turned it into more of a day trading deal. On a daily basis I would buy and if they went up, hold them. If they went against me, I'd get out. It was a very simple mechanical system back then, and it suited my personality.

Q: Can you describe what specific actions you take on a daily basis now to prepare for your trading?

ANDY: I go through all the volume numbers, look at *Investors Business Daily* or the Internet to find out which stocks have volume. I'll take a look at the charts and set them up in special tickers, so I'll be ready to jump on them if they make a move. I guess I would say the main thing I do is identify good trades by running volume filters on a selected group of stock charts.

Q: What time frame charts do you use?

ANDY: I'll start off with a 120-day chart, then use a daily chart, and I'll have a two- or three-day intraday chart as well, based on a one-minute variable. In addition, I really do a rigorous analysis of the previous day.

I've found that if you analyze your trade sheet every day, writing down what you did well or poorly on every trade helps immeasurably. Personally, when I get away from that, I usually get into trouble. So that's one thing that I would encourage everyone to do: Keep a log when possible of your reactions to all your trades.

Q: How would you contrast electronic trading with conventional trading?

ANDY: For one thing, you get much better fills. You also have more control over your trading. When you call a broker, you've got to wait. Today I can buy 10,000 shares of a stock before I can dial the number for a broker. So if you're going to trade on a short-term basis rather than invest on a long-term basis, I think it only makes sense to be hooked up to an electronic terminal. It's just cost effective. You don't have to pay brokers or agency fees. You're not constantly paying up for the spread.

Q: In your opinion, for most traders to trade professionally, do you think it's necessary to trade from a brokerage office like the one in Austin that you're in or does it make more sense to trade right from your own PC?

ANDY: I think that eventually band width won't be a problem, and when that happens people will be able to trade with a professional market maker's efficiency from their own PC. The reality is that today, oftentimes, the electronic software is not as user-friendly as it could be, because there are so many things to integrate in your trading.

If you are really trading as a profession, I think it helps to be around other traders who can provide an important synergy. You get to see and hear what other professionals are doing, assuming they are accomplished traders! You don't want to go where other people are blowing themselves up, which happens far too often with trading.

I think a lot of positives have been added to my performance by sitting around other professionals, calling out trades and talking about various market entries and exits. It gives you a better feel for the market. And sometimes, you see that added opportunity you wouldn't have seen on your own. That alone makes it well worthwhile.

Q: What specific stocks do you trade, and how do you arrive at your portfolio mix?

ANDY: I've got 450 stocks on my screen. I can't watch the ticker very much anymore with all the ECNs and the small price changes, as you can imagine. That used to be my strength. In the past, I was able to read the ticker, and I could remember all the prices on the old Nasdaq workstations, one and twos. But now it goes too fast, so I've changed my style a bit. Today, I just add stocks that look good and have volume. On a given day, I'll do 500 or 600 roundtrips, usually for about 1,000 shares apiece. I'll do a healthy mix of New Yorks as well as Nasdaqs. I should add, though, for the New Yorks the price discovery is poor.

Q: There's a different standard for the New York than for Nasdaq?

ANDY: Yes, there's the specialist system. I won't say they're out to screw you, but they certainly aren't showing the order flow.

Q: What kind of criteria have you used to create the 450-stock mix in your trading portfolio?

ANDY: Basically, it's the same thing that I was talking about earlier: Simply identify stocks that are coming into new high territory that have big volume. There are stocks that are coming out of IPOs, or whatever, that start in the 15s and go up into the 100s.

Q: By 15s, you mean price?

ANDY: Yes, 15s in price. And just as they're coming on, they're the ones with the most volatility and volume. Ultimately, they are the ones I end up trading.

Q: What about household names like Microsoft, Cisco, and the other Internet stocks?

ANDY: All those guys too.

Q: What specific techniques do you use?

ANDY: In general, I truly believe that you can pretty much buy new highs and sell new lows and end up all right at the end of the month, if you have good risk control and move quickly out of losers. It's not going to work every day, but most of the time it will, if you weed out the losers and hold onto the winners, or even add to the winners.

Q: What kind of risk are you taking when you go into a position at a new high?

ANDY: Well, that's what changes every three to six months! When I first started day trading, there were quarter stocks and eighth stocks on the Nasdaq. You had your Intels and Cascades and stocks like that trading for quarters and eighths. At the time, I would buy a stock that was, let's say, in the 80s. I'd call that a quarter stock; it was usually spread by quarters. If I bought Microsoft at 80, then a quarter stock, I would be willing to risk a ¾-point stop loss from my initial entry point if it then went against me. Now if it went in my direction for a while, I would use a 1-point trailing stop. For instance, if it got to 82½, I would sell it out at 81½. That is just the kind of mechanical process that I was speaking of earlier.

Now for an eighth stock, I'd give it ⅜ point against me. I'd take a ⅜ loss immediately if I was wrong. But when I was right, I'd give it only ½ point and go on from there. But now, of course, the spreads have been wider. And with liquidity and market makers wiggling the market, you've got to expand your parameters.

Q: How often do you find that market makers wiggle you out, and then you experience the market run for 3 or 4 points in your initial direction?

ANDY: Actually, it happens quite a bit. So you've got to get back in. Really, you can't blame it on the market makers; it's their job to make money.

Q: Of course, I certainly didn't want to imply that they were doing anything wrong.

ANDY: You know, price goes against you and you get out. Then it comes back up. So what's new? That's pretty much what happens. And really, now it seems like the market makers don't have as much effect on the market as they did because of all the ECNs.

Q: Would you say that with the 450 names you now trade you've probably had to widen the risk a bit for some stocks but not for others?

ANDY: That's pretty much the case. For Yahoo, for instance, I'll give it 5 points. Initially, if you get in right or wrong, it doesn't matter. You just need to let it have 5 points to see if you're in the right direction.

Q: And what gets you out? If the market keeps moving your way, you won't take profits until it reverses the 5 points, right?

ANDY: That's right—not until it breaks through the wiggle area, for the most part. I try to just hold on to them. I'll give up the fat on the back end in order to stay with the main part of the move. Sometimes, I end up being in certain stocks for days at a time.

Q: Because they don't reverse?

ANDY: Yes. The pros tell you that there's nothing like a big bull or bear move that lasts for three or four days. It can be pretty profitable.

Q: And you can go three or four days without a stock reversing more than a point?

ANDY: It's hard to do that. But, in general, I'm giving up more than a point today, except for the smaller stocks.

Q: So your parameters keep widening out?

ANDY: Today, there's a lot more market feel involved because the volatility is so much greater. And it's hard to see the full depth of the market. The actual spread is much wider, so you've got to expand with it.

Q: What unique considerations do you feel distinguish day trading from a longer-term approach?

ANDY: That's a good question. I think it depends on what you're comfortable with, and certainly for me day trading is great. If you're a professional, I think you must watch the market all the time. Doing otherwise can be hazardous.

Q: If you're trading 500 times a day, that's got to be a lot of turns per hour.

ANDY: Yes. I mean, I'm moving in and out all the time, preferencing market makers. I'll get into 10,000 Dells and 7,000 or 8,000 Cisco, and 3,000 or 4,000 Yahoo. I am probably in 150 to 200 names during the course of the day. I'm just getting in and getting out.

Q: Taking losses, taking profits?
ANDY: Pretty much.

Q: It's a busy day.
ANDY: Yes, it's very busy. Crazy, but it's good if you can manage the risk.

Q: We've talked about risk on the micro level. In a macro sense, how do you handle risk?

ANDY: In general, I will not take on any positions that are going against me. Anything that has posted a loss I do not take home. Other than that, I really don't think I have a whole lot of macro risk. I guess if I were long when a nuclear war hit and the market was cut in half overnight, I could be wiped out. But you know the real reason is that I don't do anything to manage that specific type of risk.

Q: But you go home long or short 100 names, right?

ANDY: Yes, and the diversification helps too. Look, if you play the numbers, over time you'll be right. If the market is going up and the stock is closing at its high, there's a good chance it also will go up the next day. Of course, sometimes you come in and it gaps open against you. I've come in and had, you know, 300 points erased in a hurry. But I've also had it go the other way or come in short a bunch of stocks, make a couple of hundred points, then flip it and go long.

Q: Can you talk about how long it took you to familiarize yourself with the electronic platform?

ANDY: It really didn't take that long when I got started. But that was early in the game when the software was pretty simple. Now it's much more complicated. There's a lot more activity to adjust to and a lot more buttons to push in order to get things that you want done. Before there were no ECNs, whereas today there is an enormous amount of information you have to learn to deal with to trade effectively. On Tradecast, for instance, there are probably 35 or 40 different functions you can use on function keys. Remember, all I really want to do is buy or sell at the market. I don't want to have to try to figure out all the different functions. But currently, there's not a lot of smart logic in the keys. I think that will come around pretty shortly. I just want to keep it simple.

Q: On average, how long does it take to learn the electronic trading platform?

ANDY: Everybody that comes in our firm goes through a small training class. We start them off trading 100 shares, and they'll train for weeks. Of course, you're the worst trader you'll ever be when you first get started, so you want to trade the smallest amount at that point.

Q: A legendary trader used to say when he was asked what he does for a living: "I take losses." That was part of a successful trader's job description. It's tough for people to understand that. What has been your most successful trade?

ANDY: I'm not exactly sure what my biggest trade has been, but I've made a couple hundred points in a trade before. Generally, my worst days will be about a third of my biggest days. And the same thing goes for my trades. My worst trade ever was a 60-

or 70-point loser. I think I made a couple hundred points in size once; I was short 20,000 shares. I made 10 or 15 points in it. I've also been stuck in 35,000 shares ripping against me for a couple of points once. I experiment a little bit and then find out my heart really can't take it. It's just too much size.

Q: How has electronic trading changed your perception of the overall market?

ANDY: In truth, I can't say that I knew anything of the overall market before I started. So I can't say that it has changed my perspective. It's really the only perspective I've ever known.

Q: What would be your advice to an aspiring day trader?

ANDY: I would find the most successful trader you can possibly find and see if you can convince him or her to teach you.

Q: Is that what happens in your trading room?

ANDY: In general, but not completely like that. I do think that success breeds success. And you're going to save yourself a lot of agony if you can find someone that's really good and have them keep you out of troubled waters. I think that it's certainly worth getting some sort of apprenticeship or internship.

Q: You mean have a mentor?

ANDY: Exactly. It only makes sense. But like I said before, success breeds success!

The following charts reveal short-term tick and candlestick price data as described in the trader interviews. Specific chart formations, both buy and sell signals, will be identified and discussed in detail in Part Three, "Technical Analysis and Day Trading."

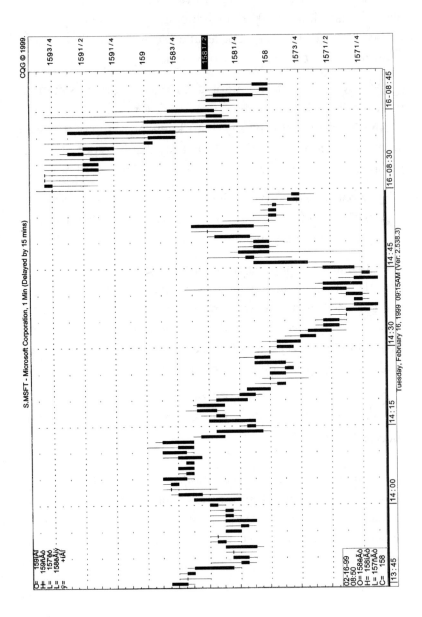

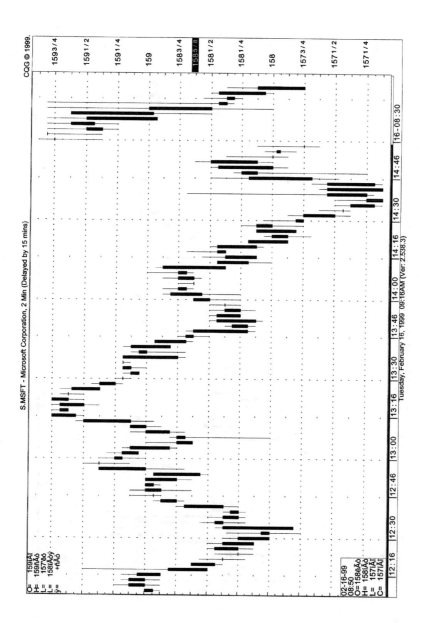

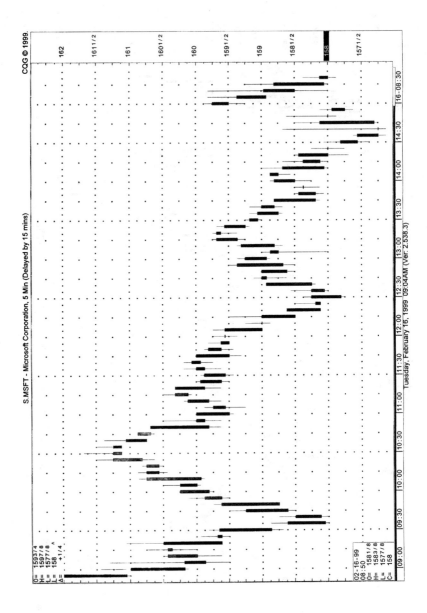

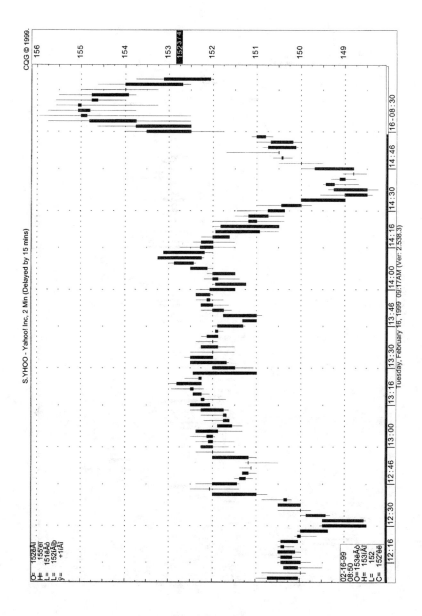

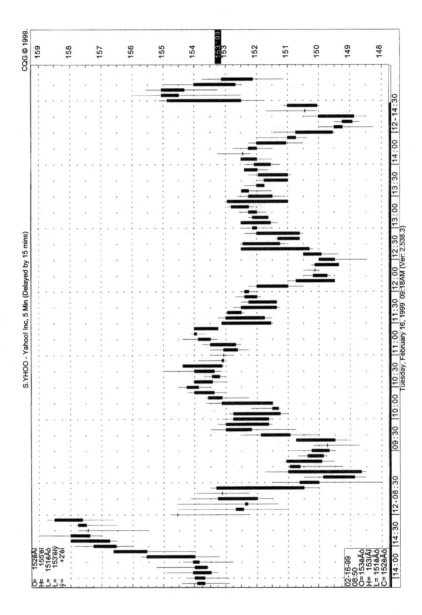

S.DELL - Dell Computer Corp. 2 Min (Delayed by 15 mins)

CQG © 1999.

O= 921/2
H= 931/2
L= 897/8
L= 933/8 V
Δ = +31/2

02-12-99
13:34
O= 921/8
H= 92'03'
L= 91'15
C= 921/8

Tuesday, February 16, 1999 09:10AM (Ver: 2.538.3)

CQG © 1999.

S.DELL - Dell Computer Corp. 5 Min (Delayed by 15 mins)

Tuesday, February 16, 1999 09:14AM (Ver. 2.538.3)

102 101 100 99 98 97 96 95 94 93 92 91 90

O=	92êÄî
H=	93nÃò
L=	89nÃò
y=	93'êéy
	+3'êî

02-16-99	
08:50	
O=	93'êî
H=	93íÃò
L=	92íÃò
C=	93êÃî

09:30 10:00 10:30 11:00 11:30 12:00 12:30 13:00 13:30 14:00 12-14:30

14:00 12-08:30 14:30

PART THREE

Technical Analysis and Day Trading

8

Technical Considerations

"The trading system gives the trader the ability to control his or her emotional states rather than allowing them to control him. A system is a disciplined method for organizing dynamic, ever-changing market phenomena."

— *Robert Koppel and Howard Abell,*
The Innergame of Trading

The stock market is a huge marketplace with well over 9,000 individual stocks from which to choose. In the following sections I present many ideas, patterns, setups, and approaches to day trading stocks. However, the beginning of a successful outcome, in my opinion, is the portfolio of stocks that you choose to focus your efforts on.

Stock Selection Criteria

The following should be your basic stock selection criteria:

- Liquidity
- Volatility
- Sponsorship

89

- Information
- Price level

Liquidity. Position traders have the luxury of slowly accumulating a favored stock even if the daily volume and participation are light. Short-term day trading requires selecting stocks that have a trading following and therefore usually have depth in bids and offers throughout the day. It can be quite frustrating to have bought a thinly traded stock just right but see the potential profit disappear because there are no immediate bids to take you out of the market.

Volatility. Successful day trading requires movement. Selecting your favorite long-term stock as a trading vehicle isn't the answer. A good stock for trading is a stock that moves in a wide daily range most of the time. This doesn't mean you have to restrict yourself to high-priced flyers or the stock in the news of the day. Many stocks at different price levels will provide you a fair opportunity over a day or two for profit. No one should select the stock for you to trade. Part of gaining an edge is being attracted to a stock and focusing on the way it moves. Because one particular stock is not active all the time, selecting one dozen or two dozen stocks to watch should provide you with frequent opportunity.

Sponsorship. Your portfolio selection should be fluid. Stocks move in and out of favor continuously. Focusing on some obscure company that you know will wake up some day is, in my opinion, a waste of time. Dull stocks that have little movement or no financial industry sponsorship are a lost opportunity and a waste of your trading resources.

Information. Stocks that move and have sponsorship usually are in the news or are widely talked about. Analyst research, rumor, merger, or a "story" creates information that helps in making many trading decisions.

Price level. Many traders select stocks on the basis of price. This is the wrong approach because the day trader is interested in movement. Yes, it's true that a $20 stock that moves a point or so has a larger percentage move than does a $50 stock moving a point or so. However, the probability of the $20 stock giving you the move you need in the short term is so small that you should look elsewhere. If the size of your trading capital is not sufficient to trade 1,000 shares of a $50 or $100 stock, then trade 100 shares or even 50 shares to maintain a trader's edge.

In the following sections I concentrate on concepts associated with day trading. Until recently, only two approaches allowed participation in the stock market. For most people in or out of the financial community, investing for the long term was the accepted method. Short-term trading or market making was the sole province of industry insiders, who were able to maintain an edge by making access to the market very difficult.

Even though, as described previously, the public now has equal access to the markets, I believe the best opportunity for trading success lies in the day swing trade. For most people, the intense concentration and discipline required to scalp for $\frac{1}{8}$, $\frac{1}{4}$, or $\frac{1}{2}$ point are difficult at best to master. The competition from insiders, who have engaged in scalping for years, and even from newcomers is formidable.

There is, however, a trading niche that makes more sense. In between the scalper or market maker and the large players who enter the market for longer time frames is the day trader. Market makers supply liquidity by scalping the spread between high bids and low offers, and longer-term players put on positions for weeks or months.

The opportunities lie in the movement of stocks over a full day or even two or three days. These moves are difficult for the large investors because large investors can't move in and out without affecting their own position. In fact, the pattern, ideas, and setups discussed here are the result of the interplay between the market maker and the long-term trader. The natural ebb and flow of price movement that we witness day in, day out offer us our greatest opportunities. Although not technical analysis in the classic sense, what follows are patterns and setups designed to put you into a low-risk trade and get you out of that trade in a short period of time.

All of the trading patterns discussed below fall into one of the following three categories:

1. Breakout trades
2. Retracement trades
3. Tests

Breakout trades.   Breakout trades occur after a period of consolidation (Figure 8.1) or after setups such as an inside day (Figure 8.2) or after a constricted-range day (Figure 8.3). Entry in the breakout trade is usually not as advantageous as in other categories but entering the market in what appears to be a strong directional bias can make up for that.

Retracement trades.   Retracements occur in the context of a trend. Buying on a pullback in an uptrend by using a percentage retracement such as 50 percent (Figure 8.4), a moving average, or a trendline (Figure 8.5) helps define the risk.

Tests.   The market is constantly testing previous price levels: two-day lows or double bottoms and tops (Figure 8.6). Here again is a low-risk opportunity to enter the market.

Each of these types of patterns and setups occurs in time frames from 5 minutes to weekly. My personal preference is a

FIGURE 8.1 Period of Consolidation

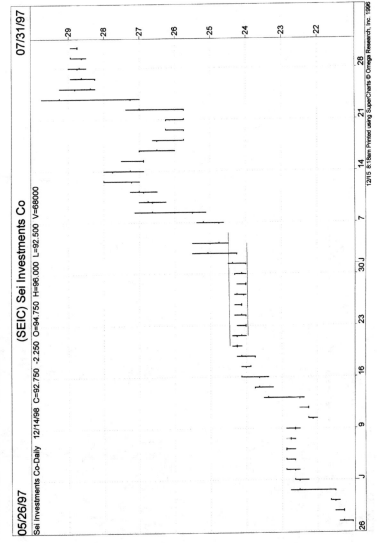

FIGURE 8.2   Inside Days

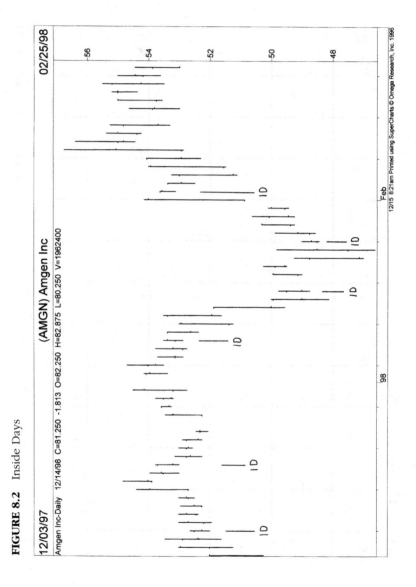

FIGURE 8.3   Constricted-Range Days (CRDs)

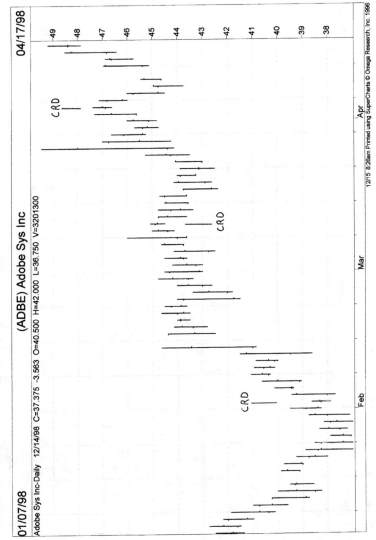

FIGURE 8.4 50 Percent Retracement

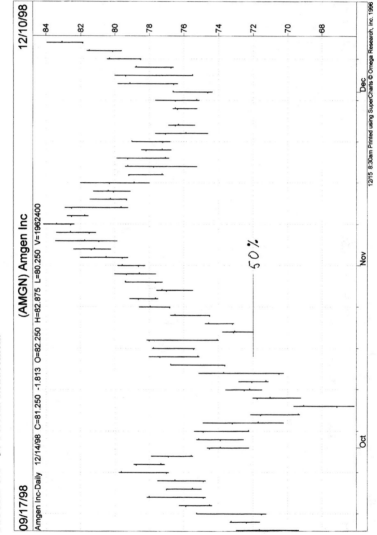

09/17/98   (AMGN) Amgen Inc   12/10/98

Amgen Inc-Daily 12/14/98 C=81.250 -1.813 O=82.250 H=82.875 L=80.250 V=1962400

50%

12/15 8:30am Printed using SuperCharts © Omega Research, Inc. 1996

FIGURE 8.5 Trendline

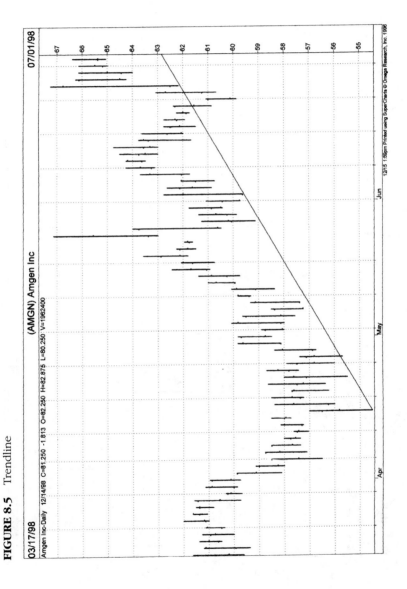

FIGURE 8.6 Two-Day Tests

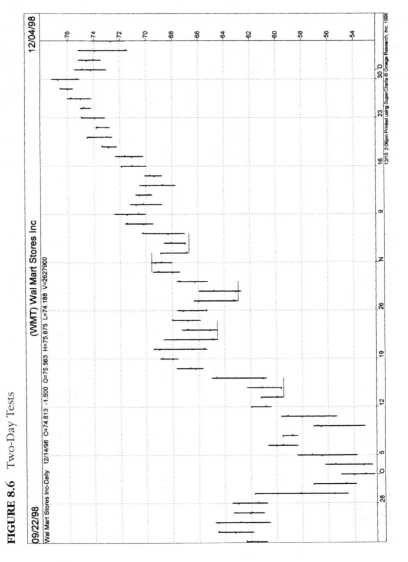

daily time frame for most stocks and a 30-minute time frame for some of the more volatile stocks.

Short-term trading telescopes all market movement and behavior into a self-imposed time requirement that enlarges and distorts the impact of the market on the trader's emotional state of mind. Therefore, day trade swing trading demands organization of thought, discipline of action, and commitment to allow numerous trading decisions to be made in the face of suffering repeated losses.

Jerry Jones, the flamboyant owner of the Dallas Cowboys football team, made his fortune in oil and gas. In answer to a question about his successful style, he recounted his early days of wildcatting: "When that telephone rings at two in the morning, you never know if the news is a strike or a dry hole that just cost you a million dollars. More often than not the news of a dry hole is followed by another phone call requiring you to commit to another project whose outcome you won't know for many months. It takes tenacity and a belief in yourself to move on." Successful traders resonate with this advice; would-be successful traders must learn its lesson!

All successful traders have tenacity and a belief in themselves. Although their methods or systems differ, their approach and state of mind are remarkably similar.

The necessary technical ingredients for a successful approach to swing trading are the following:

- Trend identification
- Market entry point
- Market exit point
- Money management

Trend Identification

What use, you're asking, is trend identification in day trading? Can you identify a trend in a day trading system? You bet! Markets exhibit consistent characteristics in uptrends, downtrends, or sideways moves. For example, it's almost axiomatic that buying lower openings in a bull market is a high probability trade. So, too, is selling higher openings in a bear market.

Trend, however, has many time frames and the day trader can incorporate and capitalize on each one that can be identified. I like to break trend down to three workable areas. The *intermediate-term trend,* usually three to ten days, is derived from what most traders see as the long-term trend of the market. The *short-term trend,* which lasts from two to five days, can be in the direction of the intermediate-term trend or a reaction to it. And the *daily trend* can result from the setup of the previous day or two, of an overnight news event, or of the morning government report.

In my proprietary trading system, we have honed the number of computer-generated numbers to just a few, which we use to identify the various trends in each time frame and which also create support and resistance within those time frames to trade against. I believe strongly in the KISS philosophy of trading: the simpler the better. So now that we have determined our trend in each time frame, we must decide on entry.

Market Entry Point

Without a plan of action—that is, without knowing where the market is in relation to where it has been—the tendency of traders to react to the emotions of the market and get caught up in the crowd increases. In simple terms, this often results in buying the highs and selling the lows, a common, painful experience! In short time frame trading, efficient entry can be the difference between a missed market, a smaller profit, or a larger-than-necessary loss.

By planning several potential entry scenarios that fit into your system, you prepare yourself for opportunities that the market offers. The most difficult thing for most novice traders to do is to buy the market as it comes crashing down to your point, number, or area. Planning and a conviction in your proven method will put you into that market. Buying a hard break or selling a sharp rally to your preplanned point is usually the smallest risk trade you can make. This applies also for buying or selling a breakout. You generally know right away if your buy or sell is a good one and, if it isn't, whether it has the least dollar risk attached to it.

Personally I try to determine if the market is set up to buy a break, to sell a rally, or, if it's in a breakout mode, to follow strength or weakness. I then place entry orders in anticipation. This requires patience.

Many times day trading appears like running for a crowded elevator whose doors are just beginning to close. Forget it! Remember there will be another one along in a minute. It's important to get into the elevator that will arrive at your floor, and that leads us to our trading exit.

Market Exit Point

Steve Conners, an investment adviser and author of the book *Confessions of a Hedge Fund Manager,* said it best: "I want my stop hit!" He emphasized this point by trailing his stop loss orders on profitable trades so close to the market that it almost guaranteed he would be stopped out, forcing him to take his money. The same attitude goes for that stop loss order. Nothing is so wasteful to a day trader as a market that wallows in a no-man's-land between a small profit or no profit and a small loss. Pat Arbor, former chairman of the Chicago Board of Trade, tells a story in *The Outer Game of Trading* (Irwin, 1994) about Everett Clip, one of the senior members of the Board of Trade:

> Everett will take a new trader and march him right down to the middle of the bond pit, and he'll say, "Now, watch this." And he'd say, "What's the market?" "Five bid at six sellers," someone says. Everett would say to the new trader, "Watch very closely." He then turns to the guy who gave him the market, "I'll sell you one at five and I'll buy one from you at six." Then he turns back to the young trader and says, "You see what I just did?" The young trader would kind of look, his eyes wide open, and say, "Yeah, you just lost a tick." Everett then says triumphantly, "That's right. Never forget it!" You see, that's how you take a loss, dispassionately, no emotion. If you can learn that, you'll be a successful trader.

You're a day trader. Take that small loss. Move on with your business!

Taking profits, on the other hand, is another matter. A sound approach should include price or some other objective for the market's performance. A reasonable price objective will vary with the volatility and risk of each individual market. For example, many systems created for trading stocks reduce the risk to $\frac{3}{8}$ to $\frac{5}{8}$ point. Under those circumstances, trying to squeeze 2 points out of the market might be a little greedy. In other words, reward should have some relationship to risk taken. There are other objectives to consider: How quickly does the market move in your favor after you enter? Something can be said for instant gratification. Also, how does the market perform as it moves toward your price objective? Is it making a new high, then backing off, and then making another new high? Or did it go into a "fast" market condition but fall short of your price objective in the middle of the day? Reacting to these differences can add dollars to any system you are using.

Money Management

Many traders confuse risk management with money management. Risk management is what we have talked about above. It is taking small losses and managing the rewards as they relate to the risks taken. Money management refers to the proper use of capital, which includes using it for maximum benefit and preserving it for maximum longevity. It makes as little sense to commit $100,000 to day trading and then trade just 100 shares, for example, as it does to trade 10,000 shares, which is too many. There is a balance to be arrived at through careful consideration of your personal comfort level, risk parameters of each system, and the volatility of the market being traded. Keep in mind that short-term trading is like hitting singles and doubles and stealing bases to win baseball games. You can win a lot of games that way but only if you have a good defense.

Whatever method, approach, or system you create for day trade swing trading, you must resolve several important issues if you are to be successful. The market must be viewed as a vehicle or tool from which your objective is to extract profits. Entering the market on your terms is your edge and reduces risk to the smallest possible level. However, as important as your entry into the market is, taking the money when it's available is a close second in importance. Trying to turn a swing trade into a home run will doom you to failure. Don't mix time frames.

You can't make a trade based on a five-minute chart and validate turning that trade into a position. Your day trading goal is to enter the market with a small risk, take your profit, and move on to the next opportunity. Worrying about what you might be leaving on the table will distort your focus and inhibit you from making good decisions. You'll find more opportunity in the markets from a sound approach or system than you'll be able to take advantage of.

Another issue you must come to terms with is the sheer number of trades you will have to make as part of your process. Believe it or not, this is a real problem for many people. Whether it is the constant decision making or the flow of paper or a stream of losses, many people fold under the weight. And this goes for pit traders as well. A clearing firm in Chicago assists traders on the floor of their exchange by teaching a proven method of scalping in the trading pit: trading for the smallest of increments throughout the trading day. The first thing traders are taught is to "scratch," or buy and sell at the same price, which teaches the traders to enter and exit the market quickly to protect themselves if the market turns. But the most important aspect of this lesson is neither of these.

The real lesson for traders is in forcing them to make trades. Yes, to just make the trades! Even when the cost of a scratch is measured in pennies, many novice traders will spend a full trading day with less than a handful of trades on their trading cards. You have to force them to enter and exit the market many times a day. I'm not suggesting that an off-floor trader should or could trade for very small increments, but the psychological barriers to making the trades are the same as for large increments.

In the following pages I show my approach to swing trading by day. I say *approach* because I believe that the essential ingredients to a successful trading method is not the system but what the trader brings to that system. By approach I mean the attitudes, emotions, focus, and state of mind that the trader incorporates into whatever system or method he or she uses. My earliest training in trading was in classic chart analysis, and I really believe in keeping it simple. That is why, except for a few computer-generated numbers that define the market's trend and create some support and resistance areas, my primary tool is the simple daily bar chart. Most of what you read here will apply in any time frame.

9

The Digital Day Trading Method

The following are some personal axioms that are integral to the Digital Day Trading Method:

- Patience is your edge.
- Good day trades result from a high percentage of setups.
- Anticipation of market opportunities is critical.
- Predetermined buy and sell areas must be executed.
- Trade one setup trade per stock per day.
- Ignore the noise and follow the signal.
- Take "fast market," or climax condition, profits.
- Abandon dull or nonperforming stocks.

Patience is your edge.   Patience and preparation serve to create an edge that helps build and conserve equity. Knowing what you expect the market to do and waiting patiently for the market to come to you—in other words, to meet your expectations—gives you that edge.

Good day trades result from high percentage setups.
Each day must be viewed in a larger context, which might be one day to two weeks of market action. Understanding how markets set up to make predictable moves and anticipating these moves through the setup is a valuable key to success.

Anticipation of market opportunities is critical.   In most instances, waiting for the stock to demonstrate what appears to be a trading opportunity will result in entering too late for maximum profits.

Predetermined buy and sell areas must be executed.
For those traders who have difficulty "pulling the trigger," putting resting orders in the market will get you into the trade.

Trade one setup trade per stock per day.   Overtrading comes from indecision and anxiety. By setting your sights on one good setup in a stock, you avoid trading your emotions.

Ignore the noise and follow the signal.   Much of what a market does during the day can be considered noise, that is, market action without meaning. Hanging on every tick can be a wearisome and misleading chore. You must eliminate your reactions to the noise and follow the essential signal.

Take "fast market," or climax condition, profits.   In day trading it's a good idea to exit a profitable trade if the market climaxes on heavy volume or "fast market" conditions. There's a high probability that the high or low of the day is being made at this time. If the market hits your resting entry orders under these conditions, expect immediate profits or be alert for another wave in the same direction.

Abandon dull or nonperforming stocks. If you find yourself in a stock that is very quiet, look elsewhere. Time is scarce and watching a dull stock drains energy.

Market Setups in the Digital Day Trading Method

The Digital Day Trading Method is based on three categories of market setups discussed below.

The Market Setup

The first setup stems from the natural rhythm of the market. George Douglass Taylor, in his book *The Taylor Trading Technique,* describes this rhythm in terms of three- to five-day swings in the market. A swing low day followed by a sell day might mean an extension of the previous day and then a sell-short day that would lead to the next buy day. Provision should be made for a strong or weak stock that might extend the number of days in the swing to five. An example of this can be seen in Figure 9.1. Understanding where the market is in the swing helps you formulate a plan for any particular day.

The Computer Setup

For the Digital Day Trading Method I use just four proprietary computer-generated numbers: a short-term and long-term trend identifier and a short-term and long-term momentum oscillator. These are represented in Figure 9.2 by the broken line

FIGURE 9.1 Market Swings

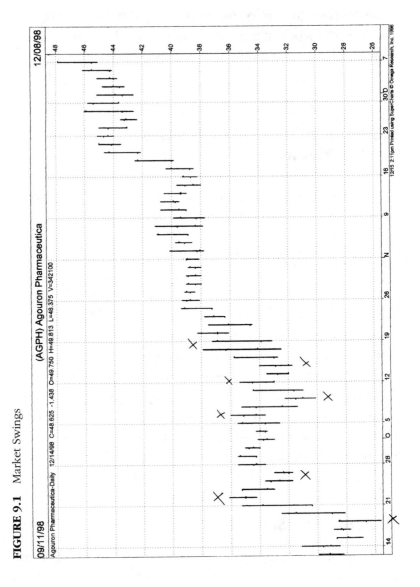

FIGURE 9.2   Computer-Generated Numbers

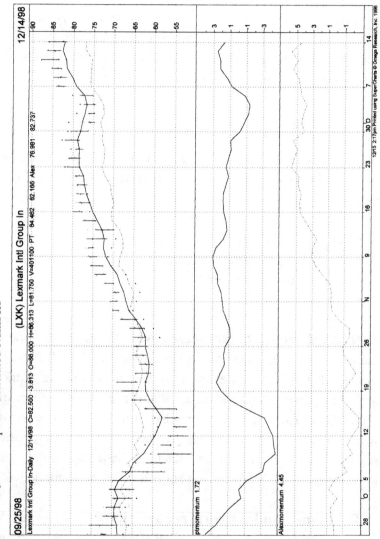

long-term trend number, the heavy dotted long-term pivot (derived from the long-term oscillator), the solid short-term trend number, and the light dotted short-term pivot.

This category can include any number of commonly used or esoteric computer-generated number that you feel comfortable using. One common error, in my view, that many traders make is to rely on this tool to the exclusion of either the stock setup or our next category, which I call chart setup.

The Chart Setup

Here I focus on using charting techniques that stand alone or are used in conjunction with our other setup categories. They include:

- Natural market retracements
- Trendlines and pattern recognition
- Daily or two-day patterns
- Highs and lows

Natural market retracements. Market retracements include Fibonacci ratios, Gann Fan lines, the Elliot Wave, and the like. Figure 9.3 is an example of Microsoft's finding support at the 50 percent retracement level and Figure 9.4 is an example of Gann Fan lines. Also included in this setup category are market retracements to moving averages. The setup of market retracements is usually most effective when the market tests these areas on buy days or sell-short days in the natural swing.

Trendlines and pattern recognition. Many times the simplest devices are the most effective, as we can see in Figure 9.5. The bottom triangle breakout leads to a flag pattern consolidation with increasing volatility and opportunity. The flags and pennant patterns are textbook. Traders may either buy the

FIGURE 9.3   50 Percent Retracement

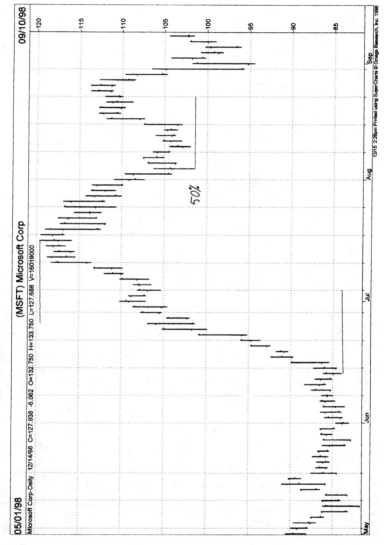

FIGURE 9.4 Gann Fan Lines

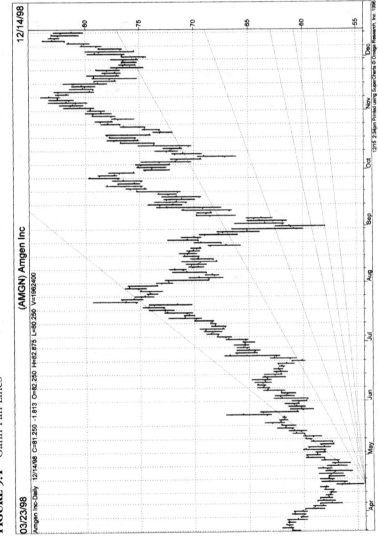

FIGURE 9.5 Flag and Triangle Patterns

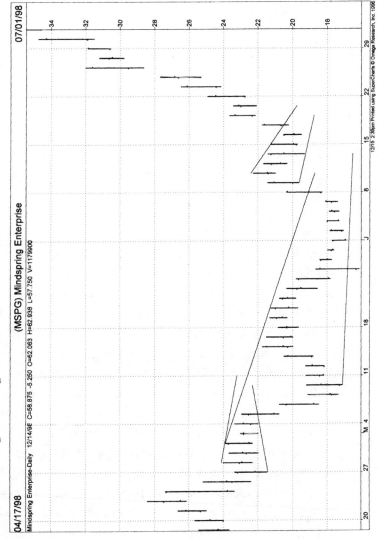

small pullbacks in the flag pattern or wait for the breakout and follow the market strength or weakness.

Daily or two-day patterns.   These patterns include the following (see Figure 9.6.):

1. An outside day (OD) is one in which the day's range is above and below that of the previous day's range. The day following an outside day can usually be traded by buying dips and selling rallies.

2. An inside day (ID) is one in which the day's range is below the high and above the low of the previous day's range. Inside days are often followed by increased volatility and should be traded by buying the breakout above the previous day's high and selling a breakout below the previous day's low.

3. A constricted-range day (CRD) is one in which the range contracts to the smallest range of the past several days. Sometimes the stock will contract over two or more days. Patience here can provide opportunity. This is another pattern where the trader should be prepared to trade the breakouts in either direction.

4. A wide-range day (WRD) refers to a range that is considerably larger than the past several days. Wide-range days are usually followed by trading-range days, and the trader should look to buy breaks and sell rallies.

5. Two-day highs and lows indicate markets that tend to test the previous day's high or low and can provide the lowest-risk trades available. When the trader can combine these tests with either a computer number setup or a chart setup, it becomes a very low-risk, potentially high-reward trade.

FIGURE 9.6 Daily Patterns

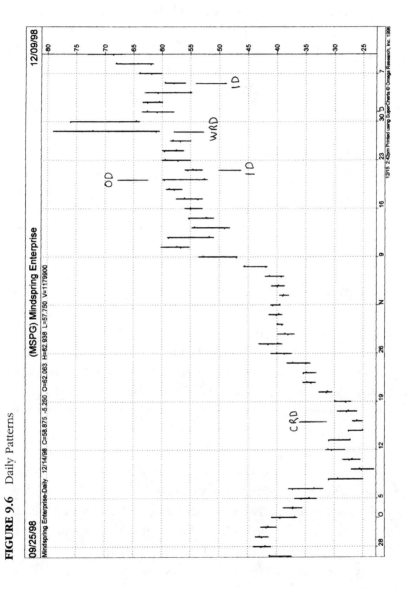

Creating a Road Map for Trades

Consistency in planning is as important as consistency in execution. Preparation and planning to be able to anticipate market action can only be effective if the trader is consistent with the various elements of his or her methodology.

Landmarks on the road map to a trade are:

- Trend
- Swing location of the market
- Pattern recognition
- One-day or two-day bar patterns
- Computer-generated numbers

Trend

The first step is to identify the stock's trend. My habit is to use simple daily bar charts with my computer-generated num·bers superimposed onto the chart. Some traders are more numbers oriented and need merely to look at a set of numbers to fix the market in their mind. Although I enjoy modern technology, I have continued to update daily charts because it reinforces a sense of continuity for each stock even though there may not have been any trade opportunities.

The important point is that the trader must determine in his or her mind if a particular market is in an uptrend, downtrend, or sideways trend. Simple trendlines or higher highs and higher lows, and lower highs and lower lows, will establish a trend. I have also included my proprietary computer-generated numbers on my charts (Figure 9.7) because they have a strong reliability for anticipating support and resistance areas of the market. As you can see in Figure 9.8, Apple Computer was well into an uptrend when it retraced and traded on the long-term

FIGURE 9.7   Trend Identification

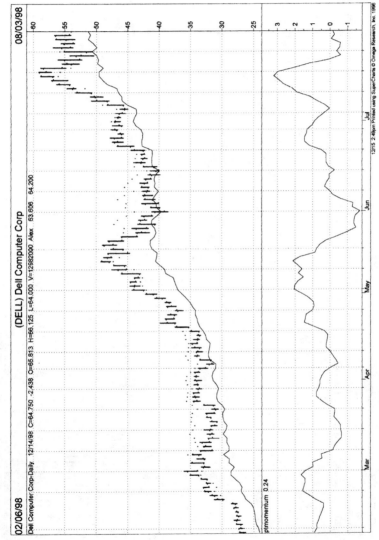

FIGURE 9.8 Trend Identification

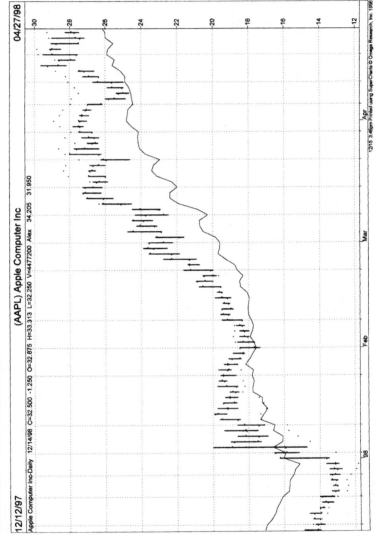

trend ID area. This creates low-risk opportunities for swing traders. The operative word here is low risk, not no risk; traders who are looking for the latter will forever be complaining about the markets that got away.

Another example of the use of trend identification is shown is Figure 9.9. This chart shows an uptrend and Fibonacci retracement numbers superimposed on it. As you can see, anticipating a retracement test of either .384 or .50 of the uptrend put you in position to make very low risk trades with large potential. In later sections we see how swing analysis and daily bar patterns help to trade this market on a swing trade basis. However, notice how the market makes it to the full .50 correction. Realistically, no one can know whether this stock goes up or down from this correction point, but we have found a high probability setup and that is all one can ask for. The point is not the specific methods shown in this section on trend identification. Rather, it is that whatever method you feel comfortable using should be the first thing on your daily agenda.

Swing Location of the Market

Determining where a market is in its three- to five-day swing pattern will go a long way to improving profitability. In *The Taylor Trading Technique* (Traders Press), George Taylor breaks down the market to a "buy day," a "sell day," and a "sell-short day." Once this rhythm is established, the trader should also pay attention to how and when the lows and highs are made each day. For example, buy days should have lows made first and sell-short days should have highs made first. For the most part, experienced traders have always sensed that morning lows in a market are a low-risk buy area. The old adage of buying a lower opening in a bull market and selling a higher opening in a bear market is still a viable operating procedure. And it is also very important for day traders as well. Morning

FIGURE 9.9   Fibonacci Retracement in an Uptrend

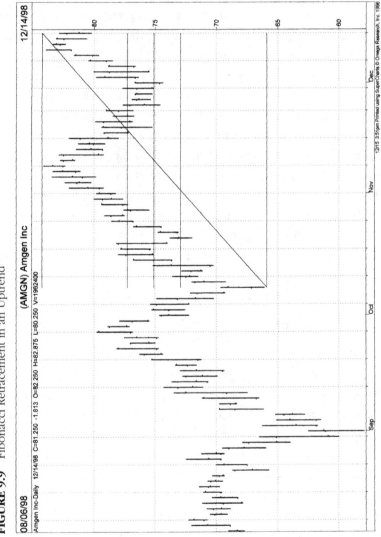

weakness into support has a good potential to react profitably as the day wears on. However, most afternoon breaks into support are not as reliable. The same, of course, goes for morning strength into resistance. So as day trade swing traders, we should be aware of the swing location setup as well as the daily setup to maximize our profit potential.

Let's follow this in Figure 9.10. I have labeled the swing high with an "S" and then counted two days for a possible buy day. The second day, labeled "B," meets our expectation of a buy day. After a weak close in the previous day, the market opens lower and makes its lows first as it proceeds to rally for the rest of the day, closing near its highs. Many traders are content, but swing traders will sell the rally that does take place on the following day (S1). The next day is an inside day (ID) and would be a sell-short day as well. CRDs, which I discuss later, will often signal increased volatility and wider ranges. This occurs the next day, which is labeled B1 and would be a buy day possibility. Don't buy weak close even on a buy day as the probability for a lower opening is very good. As it turns out, we get a higher opening or the high made first and a break for the rest of the day. It is the next day (B3) that opens lower and is the buy.

Pattern Recognition

Sometimes the most important landmarks are the simplest concepts. Trendlines that define several days of highs or lows create tests that are low-risk opportunities (Figure 9.11). The buy day bar (B) was followed by a sell day rally to the trendline, and the next day, which was a sell-short day, never violated that trendline. In Figure 9.12 we see an example of a triangle pattern and the breakout of that pattern for a day trade. You can see that the triangle formation ends with three constricted-range days in a row setting up the volatile move. Breakout moves or gap openings, although difficult to enter, often yield large payoffs. Many

FIGURE 9.10 Market Swings

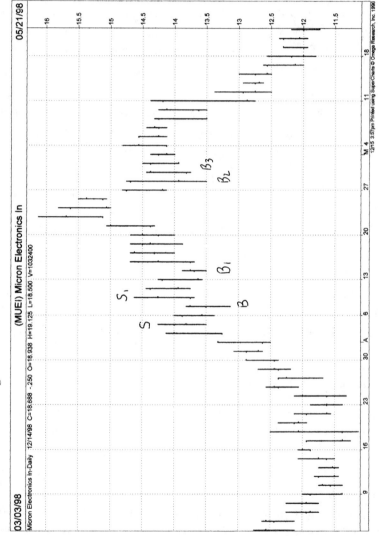

FIGURE 9.11 Market Swings

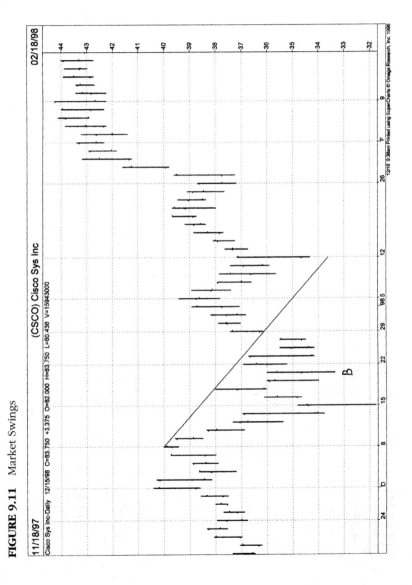

FIGURE 9.12 Triangle Pattern

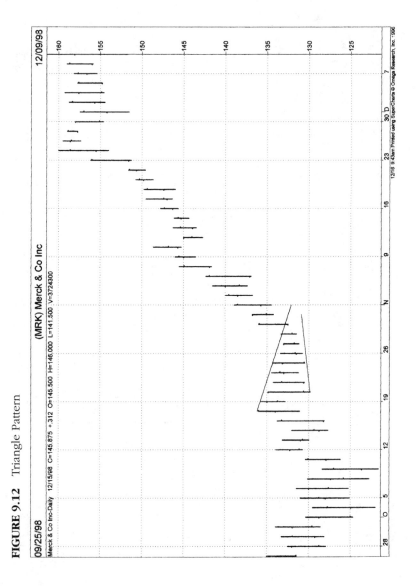

times the wider the gap opening the stronger the move in that direction. Although there is a danger of a false breakout, a reversal of this kind of pattern should be followed because of its reliability.

One-Day or Two-Day Bar Patterns

Only a limited number of possible patterns can take place in the previous day or two, but they offer us some of the best opportunities for the lowest-risk, high-probability trades. Markets seem to constantly test the previous day's high or low, and we should come to expect these tests (Figure 9.13). A strong stock usually makes a higher low, while some markets take out the previous low and snap back as evidence of probable support. If a market trades under the lows and finds no support, get out. We can also see in Figure 9.13 that the first two tests marked with an "X" were buy days or tests of buy day lows, and the third bar marked with an "X" is a sell day and a test of the previous day's high. Combining the swing rhythm with the two-day pattern can put you on the right side of the day's movement and offers the most logical entry point.

The outside days shown in Figure 9.14, which close on the ranges' extremes, usually have some follow-through that can be faded for a day trade. An outside day that does not close at the extreme of its range usually is followed by an inside day. As the market wizard Linda Bradford Raschke put it, "The market seems to use up all its bullets in one day."

Inside days are not interesting for themselves but for what they can produce in opportunity. Expanded ranges often follow inside days as seen in Figure 9.15. An ID usually indicates a breakout trade and requires some preparation and planning. Several breakout or volatility systems are published but the ideas are essentially the same. Enter at some distance from either the close or open, or high or low, of the previous bar or of

FIGURE 9.13 Two-Day Patterns

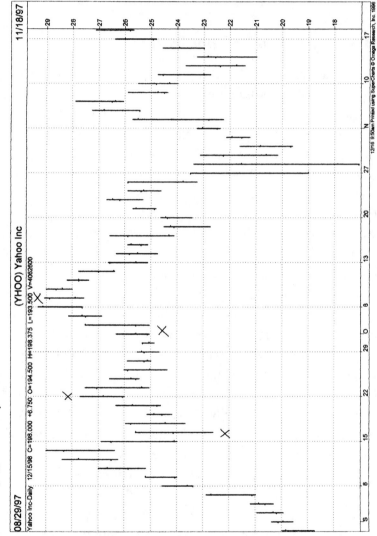

FIGURE 9.14 Outside Days

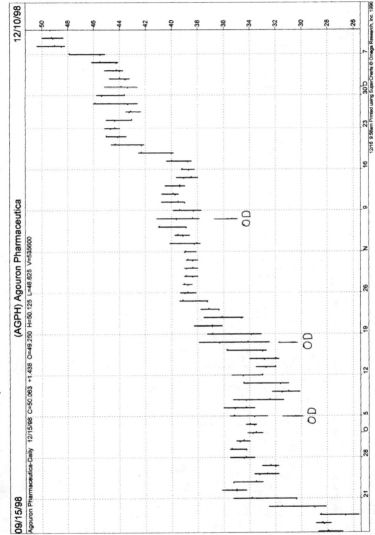

FIGURE 9.15 Inside Days

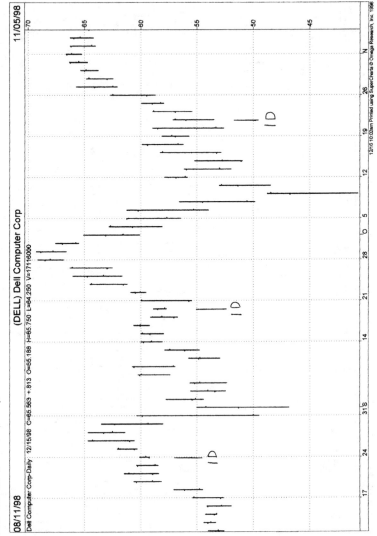

the second previous bar. I believe the high and low of the previous day works well, and, if there is a failure of the move, gives the trader the opportunity to turn around on the trade with a reasonable risk parameter.

Constricted-range days—either one or several in a row—also portend expanded ranges and breakout trades. The extent of the constriction is relative to the ranges over several recent days, as seen in Figures 9.16 and 9.17. The same methodology for breakout trades used above for the inside day can be used for constricted-range days. There are more occurrences of whipsaw action, but the narrow ranges keep the losses so circumscribed that turning on the trade and going the opposite way is a sound tactic.

I've mentioned expanded ranges several times, and it's nice for traders to be on the right side of them. However, we have seen that being aware of them offers opportunities on subsequent days so I include them as an important category.

Computer-Generated Numbers

There are no magic numbers. And certainly no magic numbers that can stand alone as a full trading system. Computer-generated numbers are a tool just as are other tools discussed previously to be used in conjunction with each other. I use three types of computer-generated numbers that are calculated for two different time frames: the trend identifiers marked as solid lines; an oscillator at the bottom of the chart; and the pivots shown as dots, which are derived from the oscillator (see Figure 9.18).

The pivot numbers are the prices the stock must continue to exceed in order to maintain the current slope of the oscillator. When the pivot moves from above to below the market, or vice versa, the market's range tends to expand and should be traded

FIGURE 9.16 Constricted-Range Days

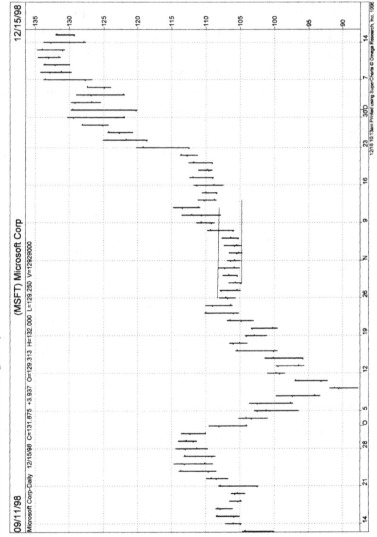

FIGURE 9.17 Constricted-Range Days

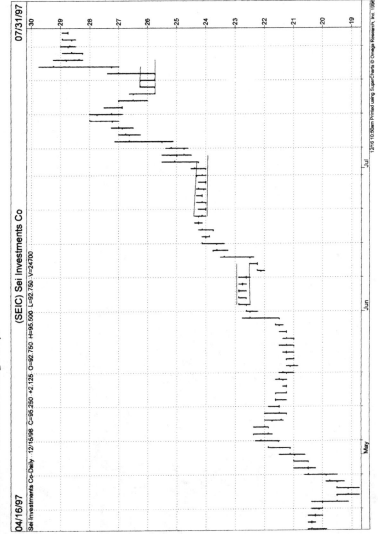

FIGURE 9.18 Long-Term Indicators

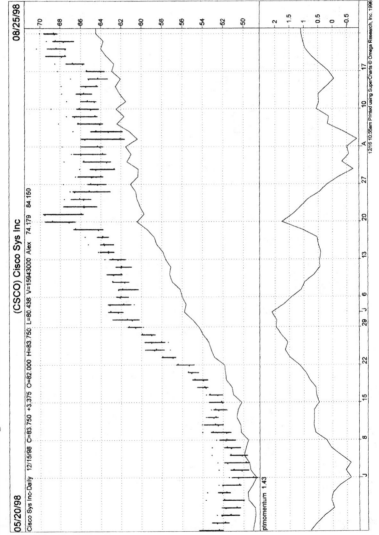

in that direction. The pivots are also reliable price points for support and resistance on a daily basis.

As a market's trend flattens out, it will trade between the intermediate-term trend price and the intermediate-term pivot. This will define the sideways trend that develops either as a continuation pattern, a bottom, or a top as shown in Figure 9.19. While this is taking place, the short-term pivot and either of the intermediate-term prices become support and resistance areas and many times define the days' ranges (see Figure 9.20).

The short term oscillator represented by the line graph on the bottom of Figure 9.21 is a very useful tool. It has definite overbought and oversold areas that allow us at Innergame to take advantage of the pivot movement and either exit a current position or take a new one at or near tops and bottoms of market swings. The oscillator also sets up divergence, which is another useful tool.

Many useful computer-generated systems are available, such as ADX, MACD, Stocastics, RSI, and Bollinger Bands among others. It is a mistake, however, to isolate these devices and trade only on their input. Each trader must find the tools that are comfortable for him or her and blend them into a methodology that fits each trader's personality. The computer numbers of the Digital Day Trading Method have been traded day in, day out for more than 15 years. During this time they have been refined, tested, and retested to ensure their reliability in different market conditions. That is where my market confidence comes from. Having said all this, I still realize they're only numbers!

FIGURE 9.19   Short-Term Indicators

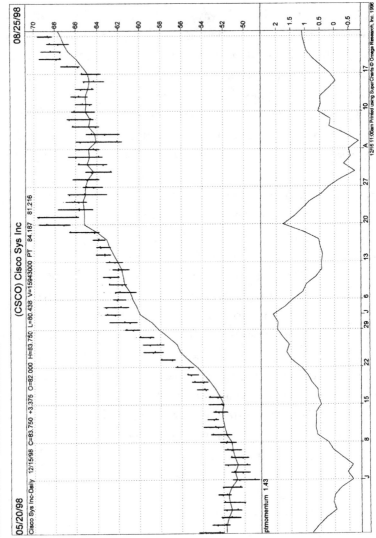

FIGURE 9.20   Additional Breakout Examples

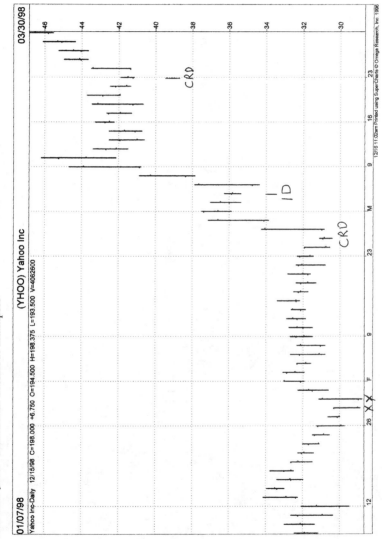

FIGURE 9.21   Additional Breakout Examples

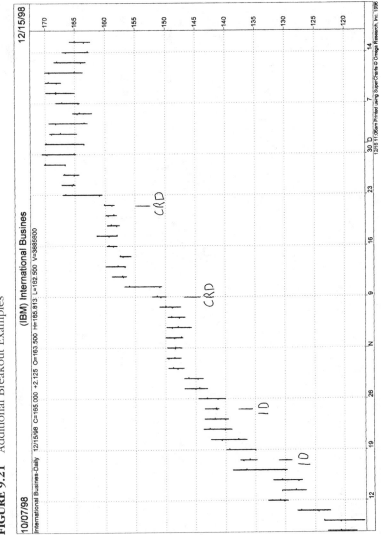

Moving from One Winning Stock Trade to Another

I've discussed all the landmarks on the road map to trading success, but we can't reach our destination if we don't plan our trip and hit the gas pedal (pull the trigger). No serious traveler goes on a journey without taking out a map and thinking through the various alternatives, obstacles, and scenarios that the trip might entail. It's the same with trading!

Through hundreds of interviews, close personal relationships with some of the country's best traders, and my personal market experience, I have never met a consistently profitable trader who hasn't prepared rigorously for trading. The most important part of your preparation must be preparing yourself emotionally, that is, psychologically and physically, to be resourceful, disciplined, and committed to whatever the market throws your way.

Remember, it all comes down to these three things:

1. Identifying an opportunity
2. Taking action automatically
3. Feeling good about the trade—knowing you did the right thing whether that particular trade is profitable or not

Identifying an Opportunity

It's decision time. You have all these tools with which to identify one or more opportunities based on probability. You have found the swing location, or a double bottom or top setup, or an inside day setup for a possible breakout. Write them down and be prepared to act!

Taking Action Automatically

You must be resolved, disciplined, and consistent in acting on your ideas and performing the necessary hard work. Every day that the market behaves as you have anticipated will reinforce your discipline and confidence.

Feeling Good about the Trade

Each trade you have made following the format outlined here is a good trade whether it turns a profit or a loss. Trading is a process and the result at the end of the process is the important thing, not each small element (individual trade) of that process. Your small losses are just operating costs that you have made to generate business. You must truly believe this and operate from this market attitude. The Digital Day Trading Method is based on this precept.

The following setups and trading patterns are day trading opportunities common to the trading floor and to off-floor trading in every market. I would now like to expand on trading ideas that I mentioned earlier through illustrations and discussion. Additional examples of tests discussed previously are shown in Figures 9.22–9.24.

Figure 9.25 shows a new high breakout of a month-long consolidation. The powerful element of this setup is the constricted-range day that precedes the breakout to new highs. Combining a breakout trade with a new high allows us to trail a very close stop as this trade should not violate the CRD low.

In Figure 9.26 the only difference is that the CRD breakout occurs after a short consolidation pattern just above the new high breakout.

Figure 9.27 shows a CRD/ID one day after a new high breakout, and this precedes a very reliable trade the next day. This

FIGURE 9.22   Additional Examples of Tests

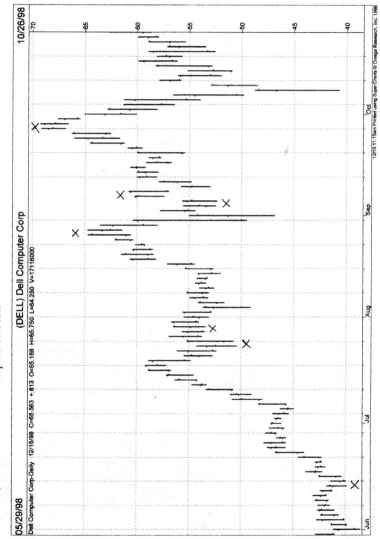

FIGURE 9.23   Double-Bottom Tests

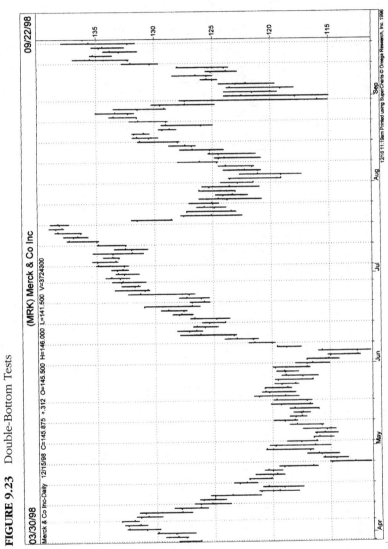

FIGURE 9.24 Double-Bottom Tests

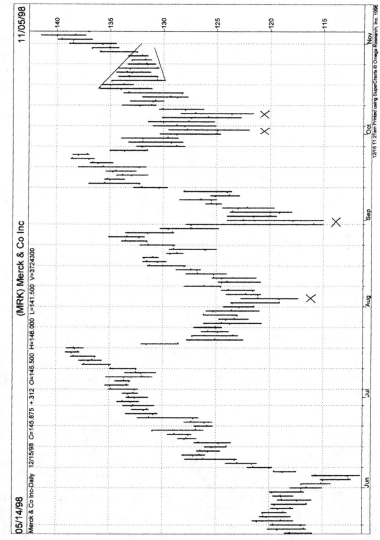

FIGURE 9.25   New High Breakout with CRD

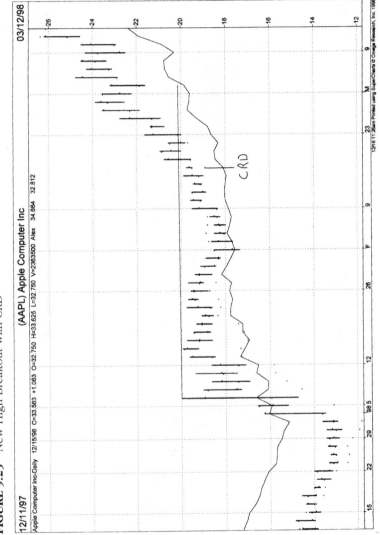

FIGURE 9.26   New High Breakout with CRD

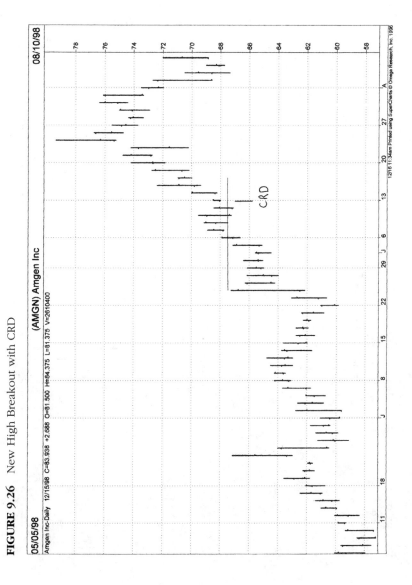

FIGURE 9.27 New High Breakout with CRD

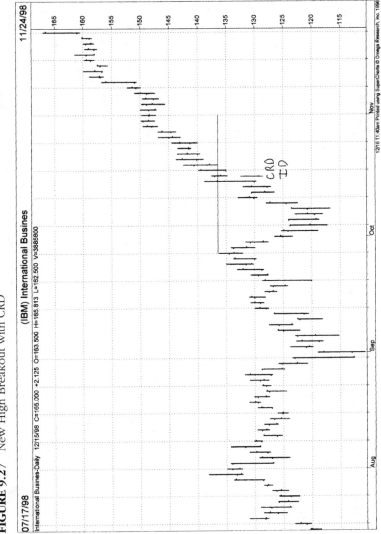

market should not trade below the ID low. Figure 9.28 is another example of an ID preceding a breakout.

The use of the breakout day, such as a CRD and ID in conjunction with other patterns, can be further seen in Figure 9.29 at the double bottom that was formed in IBM. Because we can't know if the double bottom is completed, we can use the ID as the trigger to enter the market, and the low of the move can be our stop.

If a stock is testing a previous bottom made at least five days before, then buy the stock one tick higher than the high made on the day of the test. This is illustrated in Figures 9.30–9.32.

Tops are very similar, and the trader can use this pattern to sell longs or to initiate a short position with little risk. For tops you should enter your sell orders one tick below the low of the day on which the price tested the high (see Figures 9.33–9.35).

I spoke about buying or selling on or against trendlines or moving averages. Each trader should develop a method to help him or her enter and exit the market. Two approaches that I have seen used successfully are buying or selling directly on the trendline or moving average and exiting if the stock closes below or above the buy or sell point, and buying or selling the next day above or below the previous day's range. Some examples of this are shown in Figures 9.36–9.38. Trendlines and moving averages do not in themselves compose a system, but they are very effective tools to use with other decision-making devices.

Sometimes a failed trade is the best information your money can buy. One of my favorite tactics is to buy or sell a failed breakdown or breakout. If the stock closes below the moving average or trendline and snaps back above the moving average or trendline within two days, a very strong probability of more movement in that direction is indicated (see Figures 9.39–9.41).

One of the more powerful ideas already mentioned deserves more attention: the two-day test, especially on the second or third day of a swing. Most stocks trade with a rhythm of their own. In an uptrend or downtrend a swing may extend for three, four, or five days before losing its momentum. Many times a stock will open higher and test the previous day's high by trading close to or through it. If the market falls back into the previous day's range, a low-risk trade is set up by selling the stock and using the high as a stop loss point (see Figures 9.42–9.43).

FIGURE 9.28 New High Breakout with ID

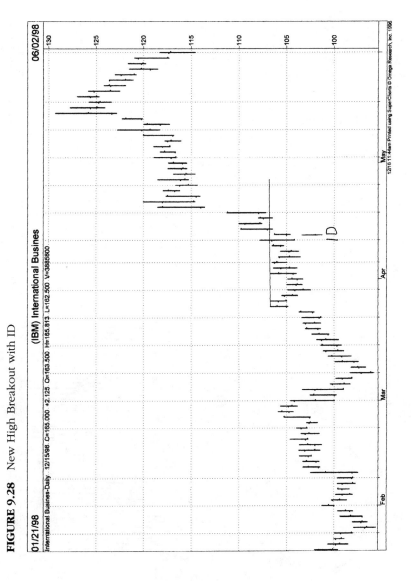

FIGURE 9.29   Double Bottom with ID

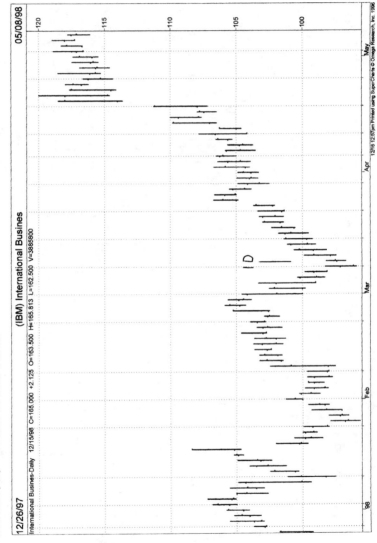

FIGURE 9.30 Double-Bottom Next-Day Buy

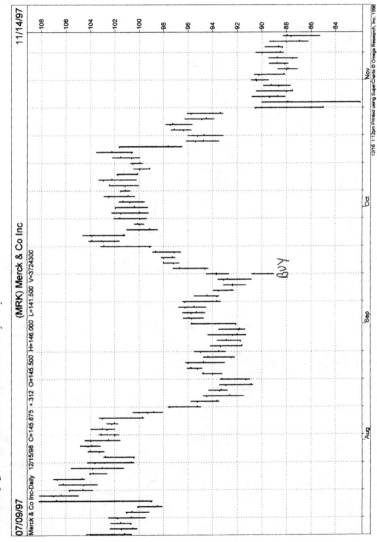

FIGURE 9.31   Double-Bottom Next-Day Buy

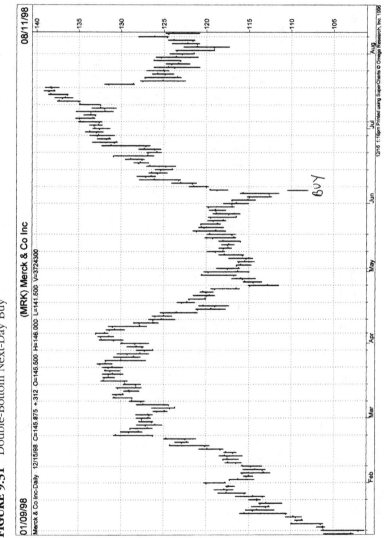

FIGURE 9.32 Double-Bottom Next-Day Buy

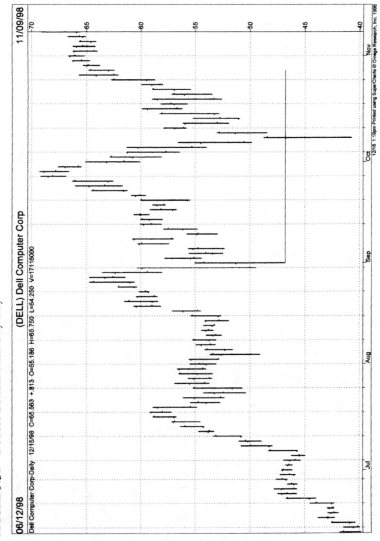

FIGURE 9.33   Double-Top Next-Day Sell

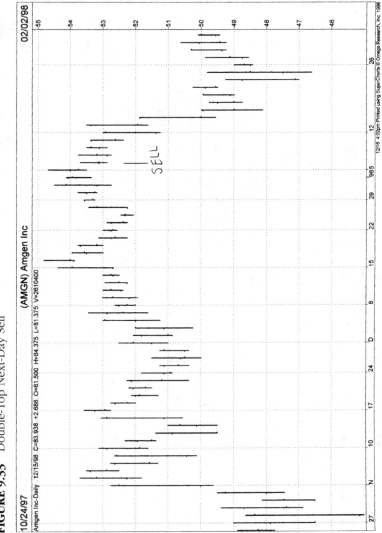

FIGURE 9.34 Double-Top Next-Day Sell

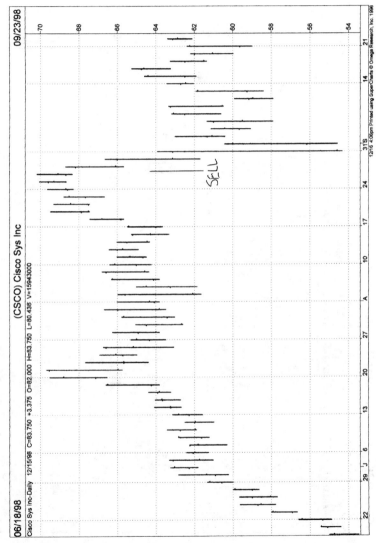

FIGURE 9.35   Double-Top Next-Day Sell

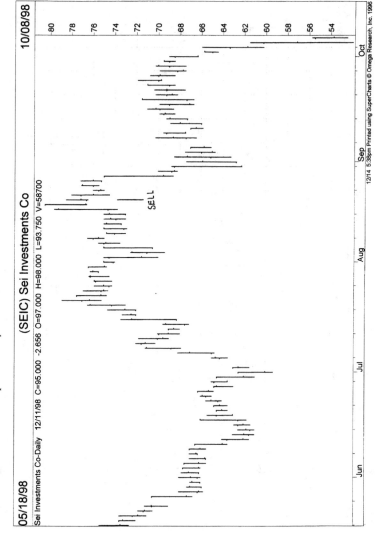

FIGURE 9.36 Using a Moving Average

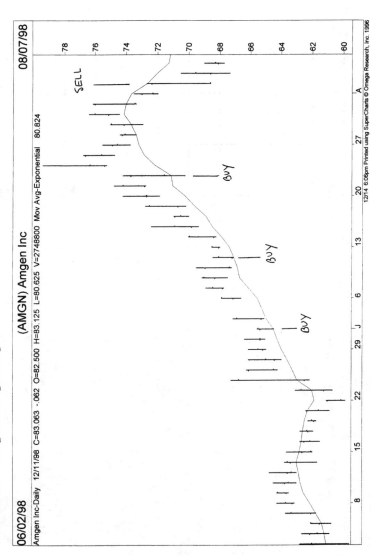

FIGURE 9.37 Using a Trendline

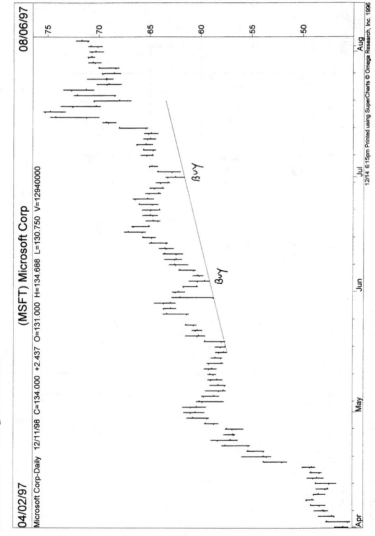

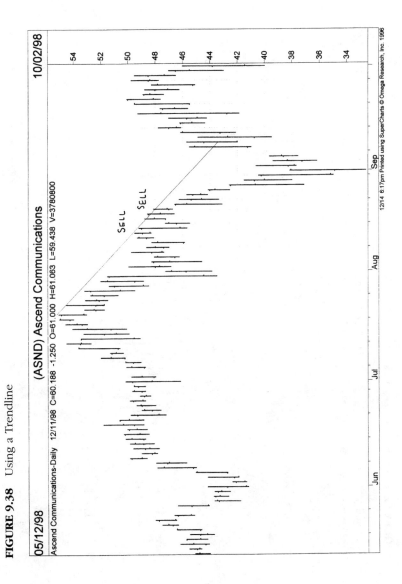

FIGURE 9.38 Using a Trendline

FIGURE 9.39 Buying the Snapback

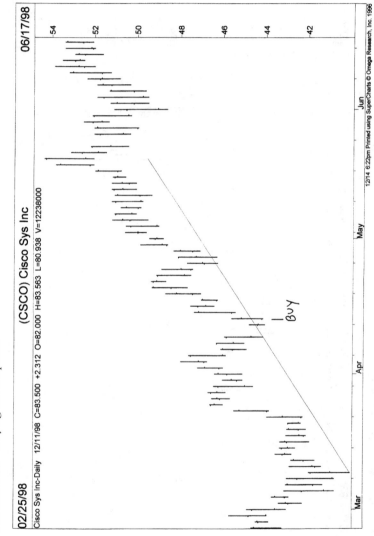

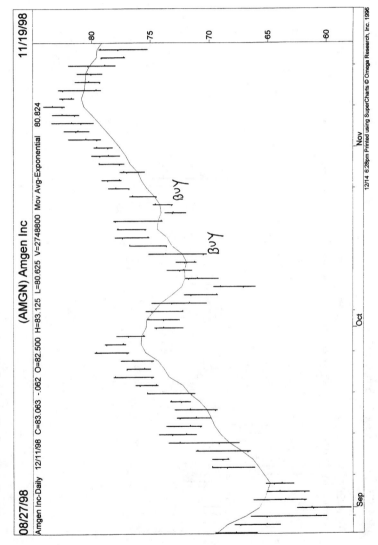

FIGURE 9.40 Buying the Snapback

FIGURE 9.41 Selling the Snapback

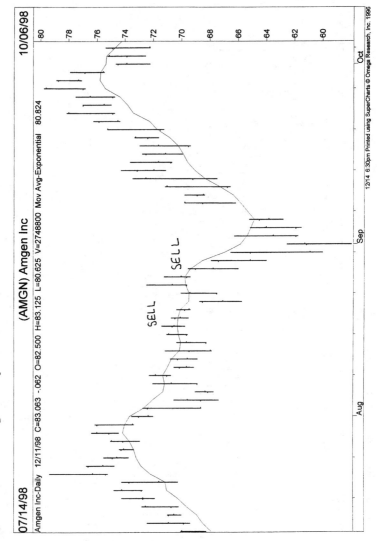

07/14/98   (AMGN) Amgen Inc   10/06/98

Amgen Inc-Daily 12/11/98 C=83.063 -.062 O=82.500 H=83.125 L=80.625 V=2748800 Mov Avg-Exponential 80.824

12/14 6:30pm Printed using SuperCharts © Omega Research, Inc. 1996

FIGURE 9.42 The Test and Reverse

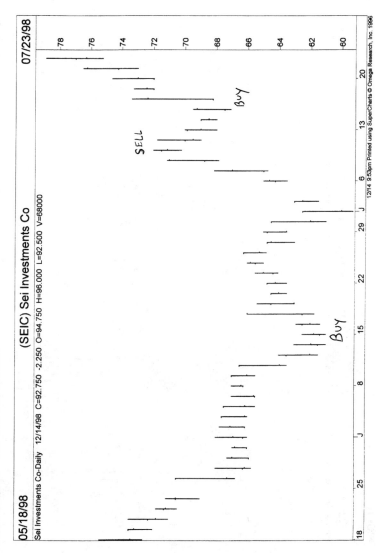

Sei Investments Co-Daily 12/14/98 C=92.750 -2.250 O=94.750 H=96.000 L=92.500 V=68000

(SEIC) Sei Investments Co

05/18/98

07/23/98

FIGURE 9.43 The Test and Reverse

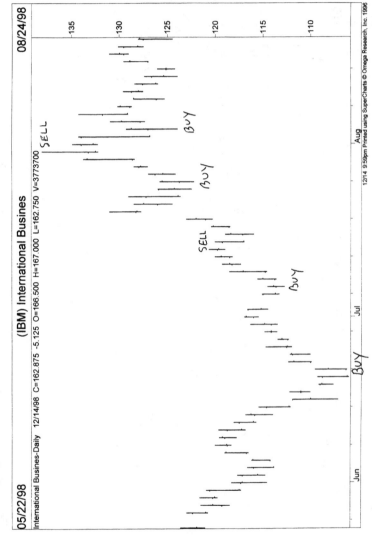

PART FOUR

Principles of Successful Day Trading

10

How Winning Traders Think

"The trader is like a Masai warrior who each day must 'face the knife' and hunt the lion with only a spear and bare hands. His success will come from relying on his own wits and instincts at the moment of truth, embracing risk as his ally to achieve the desired outcome."

— *Robert Koppel,* The Tao of Trading

Trading presents many challenges but, as with most things in life, persistence and patience, confidence and competence, and above all a willingness to pay the price will give you the desired result.

In *The Mental Game,* James Loehr, writing about tennis strategy, observes:

Many players believe they must do something very special and different on big points. As a consequence, players often break from the pattern and style of play that got them to the big point; going for too much too early is a strategy breakdown. Going for the low-percentage winner is particularly tempting on the critical points (to get the high-pressure situation over with), but generally spells failure.

Another common way of breaking down strategy-wise on big points is to suddenly start pushing the ball back, hoping

167

your opponent will make an error. Shifting to a very conservative, unassertive style on the big points in order to keep your errors to an absolute minimum will be about as effective as going for too much too soon. The old dictum, never change a winning game, still holds. Whatever you did to get to the big point, continue doing. As a general rule, you will be most successful if you learn to play offensive, high-percentage tennis on critical points. You become the aggressor and work to get your opponent to make a forced error without making an error yourself.

To do this, you must know your own game well. Your general strategy for big points should be worked out well in advance of your match: and breaking down is when you don't follow it.

This analysis is as true for trading as it is for tennis. In fact, trading could be called a state of mind, an exciting and challenging contest that is deeply satisfying and financially rewarding. Some top traders view it as an art form like banzai or the martial arts. And like these disciplines, trading requires its own discipline in the form of appropriate goals, attitudes, and strategies.

The Bottom Line

Now ask yourself the same question all serious traders must ask themselves: Do you have what it takes?

As you think about your answer, consider the positive beliefs held by the top traders:

- I believe I am or will be a successful trader.
- I believe I can achieve excellent results in my trading.
- I believe I can identify and execute winning trades.

- I believe I can trade with confidence.
- I believe I can trade effortlessly and automatically.
- I believe each day's performance is fresh.
- I believe I am personally responsible for all my trading results.
- I believe I can be successful without being perfect.
- I believe my performance as a trader does not reflect on my self-worth.
- I believe one bad trade is just that.
- I believe trading is a process.
- I believe that by believing in myself and in any proven methodology and by approaching trading each day with a fresh, positive state of mind, I possess the ultimate trading edge.

In *The Alchemy of Finance* (New York: Wiley, 1994), George Soros writes:

Values are closely associated with the concept of self—a reflexive concept if ever there was one. What we think has a much greater bearing on what we are than the world around us. What we are cannot possibly correspond to what we think we are, but there is a two-way interplay between the two concepts. As we make our way in the world, our sense of self evolves. The relationship between what we think we are and what we are in reality is the key to happiness—in other words, it provides the subjective meaning of life.

Remember that capturing the real edge in trading involves the following:

- Personal discipline based on hard work, independence, and patience
- Love of trading—making the process fun

- Well-defined risk management
- Total acceptance of losing as part of the process
- Understanding and acting on your motives for trading
- Developing a personal strategy that works for you and fits your personality
- Trading in a positive state of mind

It is just that simple, not easy, but simple. Anything else is distraction.

Miyamoto Musashi wrote the *Book of Five Rings* in 1643. It is one of the most important texts on strategy emerging from Japan's Bushi (Samurai) culture. Its insights were designed for leaders in all professions who were in search of individual mastery and achieving personal excellence. Musashi advises the following:

Think of what is right and true.
Learn to see everything accurately.
Become aware of what is not obvious.
Be careful even in small matters.
Do not do anything useless.

I have had the good fortune over a long career to have had many highly successful traders as friends. I have chosen to list below a sample of the thoughts of top traders about short-term trading. I think their perspectives provide insight into how their minds work and why they are able to trade with such successful results.

According to Joseph Siegel, "All successful trading comes down to three things: knowledge, nerve, and the ability to lose money.

"Everybody has the ability to lose money but it takes nerve to lose and then choose to stay in the game . . . to want to come back . . . to have the audacity to assume that you're smart enough to make your trade and take advantage of opportunities and make money. I found that the psychology of being able to lose money and come back was a big factor. Because it's very easy to lose money and very easy to become discouraged. You have to have a great deal of confidence in yourself that even though you've taken a beating in the market, whatever form it takes, you can come back, you can return and trade effectively.

"Any trader would benefit by learning how to teach himself to become more confident. Confidence comes from a belief in oneself based on hard work and disciplined trading. Do not overtrade! Start slowly and work your way up and don't be jealous of the other traders; it makes no difference what the others are doing! If you learn to understand yourself, you've got an edge on everyone else."

Gene Agatstein observes, "Successful trading gets right down to the psychology of self-esteem and confidence. If you're trading long enough and intensely enough, I think ultimately the statistics have to work in your favor if you just hold on to the winners and cut the losers. So why doesn't it work for everyone? The answer is self-confidence."

George Segal put it this way: "I think that successful traders have a personality, that they're not afraid to have 19 losing trades out of 20, because the 20th can be a trade that's much greater than all 19 put together. They're not hung up on losing money. They want to protect what they've got and wait for the opportunity to make a lot of money.

"They're willing to accept the loss, to take a loss and come back and make another trade, and know there's always tomorrow. There's always another trade to be make tomorrow; they don't like to take a big loss.

"There are also people who are afraid to go into trades, but they shouldn't be trading if they're afraid to get involved, even if it's only one lot. I mean I would assume a lot of people have gotten out of trading because they're afraid to make trades."

According to Linda Bradford Raschke, "My philosophy is to do whatever works, whatever makes your bottom line go up."

My number one job is to make a living, not to be a millionaire overnight. I've got to put bread and butter on the table, pay my bills. I've got to make a living. This is what I do for my job, so I need a steady, consistent equity curve. That's why I try to concentrate on the shorter-term time frame. I just like the comfort in small, steady gains.

Another thing I want to emphasize that you learn, whether you trade short term, from a mechanical system, or with a methodology like the one I teach: It's important to be consistent.

Trading is just a numbers game, that's all it is. You get a little bit of an edge in your favor, a little bit of an arbitrage, a little bit of a price pattern: anything that gives you that edge. But you have to have that edge. And then it is just a numbers game. You crank that out, you say I've got to do 100 trades, with 65 percent winners and 35 percent losers—that's my average loss. You have to get that consistency going. If you're consistently losing, then maybe it's time you get a different pattern, or a different edge, or an arbitrage. So you have to look at the long-term scheme of things.

Even though I look at my profitability every day, I'm not necessarily looking at each and every trade.

Just because I'm a short-term trader doesn't mean I don't hold trades for the long term, too. Believe me, I have put on a position and stuck with it for three months. I just don't look at the thing. I have to take it off my quote machine, off my trading sheet, out of my mind, or I'm going to want to play with it. It's like those seasonals; they drive me crazy sometimes because even though they work, I'm looking at this position and I know I'm supposed to leave it on for another three weeks, but I want to get in there and start fooling with it.

So work with what fits your style. On the trading floor, we're constantly scaling in and scaling out of trades. That's one of my big money management things now. I'm always scaling out of things. Put yourself in a win/win situation. Take some money off the board. Take partial profits. Because that way you can't lose. If it then goes against you, at least you locked in something. If it goes your way, you still have bullets to play with. Don't get greedy.

You have to define what works for you. There's nothing wrong with one time frame or another, or one style of trading or another; it's all a little road map in my head. It teaches me to anticipate, to have a plan. I watch it set up, and if it's there and doing what I expected, I'm in the trade.

According to Donald Sliter, consistency is the key to successful day trading. "One of my goals is to stay disciplined. Another is to not allow myself to get lazy. My goal is to trade every day. It's my job. I consider myself a blue-collar worker with a white-collar income . . . would you believe I have not had a losing month since November 1986! Each day I just chip away. It has gotten to the point that the chips aren't small anymore, but I still view it as chipping away. To other people the numbers are awesome. I've watched the guys who hit the home runs, and you know it's just not my style. I don't like putting all my eggs in one basket. I don't believe in that!"

Principles of Successful Day Trading

I've listed below what I think day traders should do—or not do—to ensure their success:

- Define your loss.
- Believe in yourself and in unlimited market possibilities.
- Have a well-defined money management program.
- Don't buy price.
- Don't take tips.
- Don't trade angrily or euphorically.

- Trade aggressively at your numbers and points.
- Focus on opportunities.
- Consistently apply your day trading system.
- Be highly motivated.
- Don't overtrade.
- Never average a loss.
- Take small losses, big profits.
- Don't be biased to either side of the market.
- Preserve capital.
- Think in probabilities.
- Always trade in a highly positive and resourceful state of mind.
- Act with certainty.
- Remember that the market is never wrong.

Successful Risk Taking

Day trading stocks in the new digital trading arena presents opportunity to traders that were heretofore unimaginable. As we have seen, however, age-old market wisdom still applies, and it is this more than anything else that will ensure a successful result. In short, the key point is that successful trading is a direct result of a well-disciplined approach to calculated risk taking that incorporates the following points:

- A trader effectively manages emotion.
- A trader is aware of overcoming the pitfalls of crowd psychology.
- A trader understands his or her conscious and unconscious motivations.
- A trader risks an appropriate percentage of the overall portfolio.
- A trader acknowledges personal abilities and limitations.
- A trader is systematic and consistent in approach.

- A trader stays emotionally balanced during winning and losing periods.
- A trader resists trades that are outside a defined risk parameter.
- A trader is open to calculated risk opportunities.
- A trader is analytical and disciplined in every stage of the investment process.

As you read over each item in the list of principles of successful risk taking above, ask yourself the following questions:

- How does all this relate to me?
- How do I personally experience risk?
- What physical symptoms do I experience?
- What emotions do I have when taking risk in the market?
- What do I hear in my mind's ear?
- What sensory imagery do I experience?
- What specific anxieties do I have of a recurring kind?
- What am I thinking when I take a loss?
- What do I believe about the market and myself when taking a loss?
- What self-defeating attitudes do I possess that I can overcome?
- How can I incorporate all of these principles into my current trading system?

Trading is a rewarding universe of unlimited possibilities when approached with maturity and well-managed risk. It is intellectually challenging and affords independently minded individuals the ability to participate in a personally fulfilling and profitable activity. The key to successful trading is always the same: turning a potentially risky situation into an undertaking of carefully planned, systematic, and well-calculated risk management. Knowing this is the ultimate edge for the digital day trader.

Appendix A

Major Stocks Traded: Nasdaq 100 and S&P 500

Nasdaq 100

Launched in January 1985, the Nasdaq 100 Index represents the largest and most active nonfinancial domestic and international issues listed on The Nasdaq Stock Market® based on market capitalization. As of December 21, 1998, the Nasdaq 100 Index was rebalanced to a modified market capitalization weighted index. Such rebalancing is expected to retain in general the economic attributes of capitalization weighting while providing enhanced diversification. To accomplish this, Nasdaq will review the composition of the Nasdaq 100 Index on a monthly basis and will adjust the weightings of Index components using a proprietary algorithm if certain preestablished weight distribution requirements are not met.

Eligibility criteria for the Nasdaq 100 Index includes a minimum average daily trading volume of 100,000 shares. Generally, companies also must have seasoned on Nasdaq or another major exchange, which means they have been listed for a minimum of two years. If the security is a foreign security, the company must have a world wide market value of at least $10 billion, a U.S. market value of at least $4 billion, and average trading volume of at least 200,000 shares per day. In addition, foreign securities must be eligible for listed-options trading.

Company Name	*Symbol*	*% of Index (Adjusted)*
3Com Corporation	COMS	0.68
Adaptec, Inc.	ADPT	0.21
ADC Telecommunications, Inc.	ADCT	0.76
Adobe Systems Incorporated	ADBE	0.3
Altera Corporation	ALTR	0.83
Amazon.com, Inc.	AMZN	1.26
American Power Conversion Corporation	APCC	0.63
Amgen Inc.	AMGN	1.58
Andrew Corporation	ANDW	0.12
Apollo Group, Inc.	APOL	0.2
Apple Computer, Inc.	AAPL	0.78
Applied Materials, Inc.	AMAT	1.41
Ascend Communications, Inc.	ASND	1.01
Atmel Corporation	ATML	0.13
Autodesk, Inc.	ADSK	0.18
Bed Bath & Beyond Inc.	BBBY	0.61
Biogen, Inc.	BGEN	0.91
Biomet, Inc.	BMET	0.57
BMC Software, Inc.	BMCS	0.83
Cambridge Technology Partners, Inc.	CATP	0.15
CBRL Group Inc.	CBRL	0.11
Centocor, Inc.	CNTO	0.29
Chancellor Media Corporation	AMFM	1.09
Chiron Corporation	CHIR	0.63
Cintas Corporation	CTAS	1
Cisco Systems, Inc.	CSCO	6.34
Citrix Systems, Inc.	CTXS	0.47
Comair Holdings, Inc.	COMR	0.21
Comcast Corporation	CMCSK	1.15
Compuware Corporation	CPWR	0.76
Comverse Technology, Inc.	CMVT	0.4
Concord EFS, Inc.	CEFT	0.39
Corporate Express, Inc.	CEXP	0.04
Costco Companies, Inc.	COST	0.97
Dell Computer Corporation	DELL	5.38
Dollar Tree Stores, Inc.	DLTR	0.22
Electronic Arts Inc.	ERTS	0.27
Electronics for Imaging, Inc.	EFII	0.16
Fastenal Company	FAST	0.11

Company Name	Symbol	% of Index (Adjusted)
First Health Group Corp.	FHCC	0.06
Fiserv, Inc.	FISV	0.53
Food Lion, Inc.	FDLNB	0.21
FORE Systems, Inc.	FORE	0.16
Genzyme General	GENZ	0.59
Herman Miller, Inc.	MLHR	0.11
Immunex Corporation	IMNX	0.77
Intel Corporation	INTC	8.5
Intuit Inc.	INTU	0.71
Jacor Communications, Inc.	JCOR	0.41
KLA-Tencor Corporation	KLAC	0.67
Level 3 Communications, Inc.	LVLT	1.38
Lincare Holdings Inc.	LNCR	0.19
Linear Technology Corporation	LLTC	1.08
LM Ericsson Telephone Company	ERICY	0.93
Maxim Integrated Products, Inc.	MXIM	0.94
McCormick & Company, Incorporated	MCCRK	0.17
MCI WORLDCOM, Inc.	WCOM	5.75
McLeodUSA Incorporated	MCLD	0.2
Microchip Technology Incorporated	MCHP	0.14
Micron Electronics, Inc.	MUEI	0.12
Microsoft Corporation	MSFT	15.64
Molex Incorporated	MOLX	0.24
Netscape Communications Corporation	NSCP	0.93
Network Associates, Inc.	NETA	0.69
Nextel Communications, Inc.	NXTL	1.22
Nordstrom, Inc.	NOBE	1
Northwest Airlines Corporation	NWAC	0.17
Novell, Inc.	NOVL	0.86
NTL Incorporated	NTLI	0.52
Oracle Corporation	ORCL	2.56
PACCAR Inc.	PCAR	0.43
PacifiCare Health Systems, Inc.	PHSYB	0.21
PanAmSat Corporation	SPOT	0.86
Parametric Technology Corporation	PMTC	0.57
Paychex, Inc.	PAYX	0.77
PeopleSoft, Inc.	PSFT	0.69
QUALCOMM Incorporated	QCOM	0.65
Quantum Corporation	QNTM	0.5

Company Name	Symbol	% of Index (Adjusted)
Quintiles Transnational Corp.	QTRN	0.59
Qwest Communications International Inc.	QWST	1.14
Reuters Group PLC	RTRSY	0.27
Rexall Sundown, Inc.	RXSD	0.06
Ross Stores, Inc.	ROST	0.17
Sanmina Corporation	SANM	0.39
Sigma-Aldrich Corporation	SIAL	0.32
Smurfit-Stone Container Corporation	SSCC	0.41
Staples, Inc.	SPLS	0.97
Starbucks Corporation	SBUX	0.68
Stewart Enterprises, Inc.	STEI	0.14
Sun Microsystems, Inc.	SUNW	1.9
Synopsys, Inc.	SNPS	0.46
Tech Data Corporation	TECD	0.12
Tele-Communications, Inc.	TCOMA	1.64
Tellabs, Inc.	TLAB	0.95
USA Networks, Inc.	USAI	0.59
VERITAS Software Corporation	VRTS	0.42
Vitesse Semiconductor Corporation	VTSS	0.44
Worthington Industries, Inc.	WTHG	0.1
Xilinx, Inc.	XLNX	0.83
Yahoo! Inc.	YHOO	1.66

S&P 500

Symbol	S&P Group	Exchange	Issue Name
$SPX			S&P Stock Index
COMS	Industrial	NASD	3COM CORP
ABT	Industrial	NYSE	ABBOTT LABS
ADBE	Industrial	NASD	ADOBE SYSTEMS
AMD	Industrial	NYSE	ADVANCED MICRO DEVICES
ANV	Industrial	NYSE	AEROQUIP-VICKERS INC
AES	Utilities	NYSE	AES CORP
AET	Financial	NYSE	AETNA INC

Symbol	S&P Group	Exchange	Issue Name
APD	Industrial	NYSE	AIR PRODUCTS & CHEMICALS
ATI	Industrial	NYSE	AIRTOUCH COMMUNICATIONS
ACV	Industrial	NYSE	ALBERTO-CULVER
ABS	Industrial	NYSE	ALBERTSON'S
AL	Industrial	NYSE	ALCAN ALUMINUM LTD
AA	Industrial	NYSE	ALCOA INC
ALT	Industrial	NYSE	ALLEGHENY TELEDYNE INC
AGN	Industrial	NYSE	ALLERGAN INC
ALD	Industrial	NYSE	ALLIEDSIGNAL INC
ALL	Financial	NYSE	ALLSTATE CORP
AT	Industrial	NYSE	ALLTEL CORP DEL
AZA	Industrial	NYSE	ALZA CORP
AHC	Industrial	NYSE	AMERADA HESS CORP
AEE	Utilities	NYSE	AMEREN CORP
AOL	Industrial	NYSE	AMERICA ONLINE
AEP	Utilities	NYSE	AMERICAN ELEC PWR CO INC
AXP	Financial	NYSE	AMERICAN EXPRESS CO
AGC	Financial	NYSE	AMERICAN GENERAL CORP
AM	Industrial	NYSE	AMERICAN GREETINGS CL A
AHP	Industrial	NYSE	AMERICAN HOME PRODS CORP
AIG	Financial	NYSE	AMERICAN INTL GROUP INC
ASC	Industrial	NYSE	AMERICAN STORES CO
AIT	Utilities	NYSE	AMERITECH CORP DE
AMGN	Industrial	NASD	AMGEN INC
AMP	Industrial	NYSE	AMP INC PENNSYLVANIA
AMR	Transportation	NYSE	AMR CORP
APC	Industrial	NYSE	ANADARKO PETROLEUM
ANDW	Industrial	NASD	ANDREW CORP
BUD	Industrial	NYSE	ANHEUSER BUSCH COS INC
AOC	Financial	NYSE	AON CORP
APA	Industrial	NYSE	APACHE CORP

Symbol	*S&P Group*	*Exchange*	*Issue Name*
AAPL	Industrial	NASD	APPLE COMPUTER INC
AMAT	Industrial	NASD	APPLIED MATERIALS INC
ADM	Industrial	NYSE	ARCHER DANIELS MIDLAND CO
ACK	Industrial	NYSE	ARMSTRONG WORLD INDS INC
AR	Industrial	NYSE	ASARCO INC
ASND	Industrial	NASD	ASCEND COMMUNICATIONS
ASH	Industrial	NYSE	ASHLAND INC
AFS	Financial	NYSE	ASSOCIATES FIRST CAPITAL
T	Industrial	NYSE	AT&T CORP
ARC	Industrial	NYSE	ATLANTIC RICHFIELD CO
ADSK	Industrial	NASD	AUTODESK INC
AUD	Industrial	NYSE	AUTOMATIC DATA PROCSG INC
AZO	Industrial	NYSE	AUTOZONE
AVY	Industrial	NYSE	AVERY DENNISON CORP
AVP	Industrial	NYSE	AVON PRODUCTS INC
BHI	Industrial	NYSE	BAKER HUGHES INC
BLL	Industrial	NYSE	BALL CORP
BGE	Utilities	NYSE	BALTIMORE G & E C
BK	Financial	NYSE	BANK OF NEW YORK
ONE	Financial	NYSE	BANK ONE CORP
BAC	Financial	NYSE	BANKAMERICA CORP
BKB	Financial	NYSE	BANKBOSTON CORP
BT	Financial	NYSE	BANKERS TRUST N Y CORP
BCR	Industrial	NYSE	BARD C R INC
ABX	Industrial	NYSE	BARRICK GOLD CORP
BMG	Industrial	NYSE	BATTLE MOUNTAIN GOLD
BOL	Industrial	NYSE	BAUSCH & LOMB INC
BAX	Industrial	NYSE	BAXTER INTERNATIONAL INC
BBT	Financial	NYSE	BB&T CORP
BSC	Financial	NYSE	BEAR STEARNS COS
BDX	Industrial	NYSE	BECTON DICKINSON & CO

Symbol	S&P Group	Exchange	Issue Name
BEL	Utilities	NYSE	BELL ATLANTIC CORP
BLS	Utilities	NYSE	BELLSOUTH CORP
BMS	Industrial	NYSE	BEMIS CO INC
BFO	Industrial	NYSE	BESTFOODS INC
BS	Industrial	NYSE	BETHLEHEM STEEL CORP
BMET	Industrial	NASD	BIOMET INC
BDK	Industrial	NYSE	BLACK & DECKER CORP
HRB	Industrial	NYSE	BLOCK H & R INC
BMCS	Industrial	NASD	BMC SOFTWARE
BA	Industrial	NYSE	BOEING CO
BCC	Industrial	NYSE	BOISE CASCADE CORP
BSX	Industrial	NYSE	BOSTON SCIENTIFIC CORP
BGG	Industrial	NYSE	BRIGGS & STRATTON CORP
BMY	Industrial	NYSE	BRISTOL MYERS SQUIBB CO
BF/B	Industrial	NYSE	BROWN-FORMAN CORP
BFI	Industrial	NYSE	BROWNING FERRIS INDS INC
BC	Industrial	NYSE	BRUNSWICK CORP
BNI	Transportation	NYSE	BURLINGTON NTHRN SANTA FE
BR	Industrial	NYSE	BURLINGTON RESOURCES INC
CS	Industrial	NYSE	CABLETRON SYSTEMS
CPB	Industrial	NYSE	CAMPBELL SOUP CO
COF	Financial	NYSE	CAPITAL ONE FINANCIAL
CAH	Industrial	NYSE	CARDINAL HEALTH, INC
CCL	Industrial	NYSE	CARNIVAL CORP
CPL	Utilities	NYSE	CAROLINA POWER & LIGHT CO
CSE	Industrial	NYSE	CASE CORP
CAT	Industrial	NYSE	CATERPILLAR INC
CBS	Industrial	NYSE	CBS CORP
CD	Industrial	NYSE	CENDANT CORPORATION
CTX	Industrial	NYSE	CENTEX CORP
CSR	Utilities	NYSE	CENTRAL & SOUTH WEST CORP

Symbol	S&P Group	Exchange	Issue Name
CEN	Industrial	NYSE	CERIDIAN CORP
CHA	Industrial	NYSE	CHAMPION INTL CORP
SCH	Financial	NYSE	CHARLES SCHWAB
CMB	Financial	NYSE	CHASE MANHATTAN CORP
CHV	Industrial	NYSE	CHEVRON CORP
CB	Financial	NYSE	CHUBB CORP
CI	Financial	NYSE	CIGNA CORP
CINF	Financial	NASD	CINCINNATI FINANCIAL
CIN	Utilities	NYSE	CINERGY CORP
CC	Industrial	NYSE	CIRCUIT CITY STORES INC
CSCO	Industrial	NASD	CISCO SYSTEMS INC
C	Financial	NYSE	CITIGROUP INC
CCU	Industrial	NYSE	CLEAR CHANNEL COMMUNICATIONS
CLX	Industrial	NYSE	CLOROX CO
CGP	Utilities	NYSE	COASTAL CORP
KO	Industrial	NYSE	COCA COLA CO
CCE	Industrial	NYSE	COCA-COLA ENTERPRISES
CL	Industrial	NYSE	COLGATE PALMOLIVE CO
CG	Utilities	NYSE	COLUMBIA ENERGY GROUP
COL	Industrial	NYSE	COLUMBIA HCA HLTHCRE CORP
CMCSK	Industrial	NASD	COMCAST CORP
CMA	Financial	NYSE	COMERICA INC
CPQ	Industrial	NYSE	COMPAQ COMPUTER CORP
CA	Industrial	NYSE	COMPUTER ASSC INTL INC
CSC	Industrial	NYSE	COMPUTER SCIENCES CORP
CPWR	Industrial	NASD	COMPUWARE CORP
CAG	Industrial	NYSE	CONAGRA INC
CNC	Financial	NYSE	CONSECO INC
ED	Utilities	NYSE	CONSOLIDATED EDISON CO

Symbol	S&P Group	Exchange	Issue Name
CNG	Utilities	NYSE	CONSOLIDATED NAT GAS CO
CNS	Industrial	NYSE	CONSOLIDATED STORES
CBE	Industrial	NYSE	COOPER INDUSTRIES INC
CTB	Industrial	NYSE	COOPER TIRE & RUBBER CO
ACCOB	Industrial	NASD	COORS ADOLPH CO
GLW	Industrial	NYSE	CORNING INC
COST	Industrial	NASD	COSTCO CO
CCR	Financial	NYSE	COUNTRYWIDE CREDIT INDUSTRIES
CR	Industrial	NYSE	CRANE CO
CCK	Industrial	NYSE	CROWN CORK & SEAL INC PA
CSX	Transportation	NYSE	CSX CORP
CUM	Industrial	NYSE	CUMMINS ENGINE CO INC
CVS	Industrial	NYSE	CVS CORP
CYM	Industrial	NYSE	CYPRUS AMAX MINERALS CO
DCN	Industrial	NYSE	DANA CORP
DHR	Industrial	NYSE	DANAHER CORP
DRI	Industrial	NYSE	DARDEN RESTAURANTS
DGN	Industrial	NYSE	DATA GENERAL CORP
DH	Industrial	NYSE	DAYTON HUDSON CORP
DE	Industrial	NYSE	DEERE & CO
DELL	Industrial	NASD	DELL COMPUTER
DAL	Transportation	NYSE	DELTA AIR LINES INC
DLX	Industrial	NYSE	DELUXE CORP
DDS	Industrial	NYSE	DILLARD DEPT STORES CL A
DG	Industrial	NYSE	DOLLAR GENERAL
D	Utilities	NYSE	DOMINION RESOURCES INC VA
DNY	Industrial	NYSE	DONNELLEY R R & SONS CO
DOV	Industrial	NYSE	DOVER CORP
DOW	Industrial	NYSE	DOW CHEMICAL CO
DJ	Industrial	NYSE	DOW JONES & CO INC

Symbol	S&P Group	Exchange	Issue Name
DTE	Utilities	NYSE	DTE ENERGY CO
DD	Industrial	NYSE	DU PONT (E.I.)
DUK	Utilities	NYSE	DUKE ENERGY
DNB	Industrial	NYSE	DUN & BRADSTREET CORP
EGG	Industrial	NYSE	E G & G INC
EFU	Utilities	NYSE	EASTERN ENTERPRISES
EMN	Industrial	NYSE	EASTMAN CHEMICAL CO
EK	Industrial	NYSE	EASTMAN KODAK CO
ETN	Industrial	NYSE	EATON CORP
ECL	Industrial	NYSE	ECOLAB INC
EIX	Utilities	NYSE	EDISON INTERNATIONAL INC
EDS	Industrial	NYSE	ELECTRONIC DATA SYSTEMS
EMC	Industrial	NYSE	EMC CORP
EMR	Industrial	NYSE	EMERSON ELECTRIC CO
EC	Industrial	NYSE	ENGELHARD CORP
ENE	Utilities	NYSE	ENRON CORP
ETR	Utilities	NYSE	ENTERGY CORP
EFX	Financial	NYSE	EQUIFAX INC
XON	Industrial	NYSE	EXXON CORP
FNM	Financial	NYSE	FANNIE MAE
FDX	Transportation	NYSE	FEDERAL EXPRESS CORP
FRE	Financial	NYSE	FEDERAL HOME LOAN MTG
FD	Industrial	NYSE	FEDERATED DEPT STORES DE
FITB	Financial	NASD	FIFTH THIRD BANCORP
FDC	Industrial	NYSE	FIRST DATA CORP
FTU	Financial	NYSE	FIRST UNION CORP
FSR	Financial	NYSE	FIRSTAR CORPORATION
FE	Utilities	NYSE	FIRSTENERGY CORP
FLT	Financial	NYSE	FLEET FINANCIAL GROUP
FLE	Industrial	NYSE	FLEETWOOD ENTERPRISES INC
FLR	Industrial	NYSE	FLUOR CORP
FMC	Industrial	NYSE	FMC CORP
F	Industrial	NYSE	FORD MOTOR CO

Symbol	S&P Group	Exchange	Issue Name
FJ	Industrial	NYSE	FORT JAMES CORP
FO	Industrial	NYSE	FORTUNE BRANDS, INC
FWC	Industrial	NYSE	FOSTER WHEELER CORP
FPL	Utilities	NYSE	FPL GROUP INC
BEN	Financial	NYSE	FRANKLIN RESOURCES INC
FCX	Industrial	NYSE	FREEPORT-MCMORAN COPPER & GOLD
FRO	Utilities	NYSE	FRONTIER CORP
FTL	Industrial	NYSE	FRUIT OF THE LOOM
GCI	Industrial	NYSE	GANNETT CO INC
GPS	Industrial	NYSE	GAP INC
GTW	Industrial	NYSE	GATEWAY 2000 INC
GD	Industrial	NYSE	GENERAL DYNAMICS CORP
GE	Industrial	NYSE	GENERAL ELECTRIC CO
GIC	Industrial	NYSE	GENERAL INSTRUMENT CORP
GIS	Industrial	NYSE	GENERAL MILLS INC
GM	Industrial	NYSE	GENERAL MOTORS CORP
GPC	Industrial	NYSE	GENUINE PARTS CO
GP	Industrial	NYSE	GEORGIA PACIFIC CORP
G	Industrial	NYSE	GILLETTE CO
GDW	Financial	NYSE	GOLDEN WEST FINANCIAL
GR	Industrial	NYSE	GOODRICH B F CO
GT	Industrial	NYSE	GOODYEAR TIRE & RUBBER CO
GPU	Utilities	NYSE	GPU INC
GRA	Industrial	NYSE	GRACE W R & CO HLDG CO
GWW	Industrial	NYSE	GRAINGER W W INC
GAP	Industrial	NYSE	GREAT ATLANTIC & PAC TEA
GLK	Industrial	NYSE	GREAT LAKES CHEMICAL CORP
GTE	Utilities	NYSE	GTE CORP
GDT	Industrial	NYSE	GUIDANT CORP
HAL	Industrial	NYSE	HALLIBURTON CO

Symbol	S&P Group	Exchange	Issue Name
H	Industrial	NYSE	HARCOURT GENERAL INC
HPH	Industrial	NYSE	HARNISCHFEGER INDS INC
HET	Industrial	NYSE	HARRAHS ENT INC
HRS	Industrial	NYSE	HARRIS CORP
HIG	Financial	NYSE	HARTFORD FINANCIAL SVC GP
HAS	Industrial	AMEX	HASBRO INC
HBOC	Industrial	NASD	HBO & COMPANY
HCR	Industrial	NYSE	HCR MANOR CARE
HRC	Industrial	NYSE	HEALTHSOUTH CORP
HNZ	Industrial	NYSE	HEINZ H J CO
HP	Industrial	NYSE	HELMERICH & PAYNE INC
HPC	Industrial	NYSE	HERCULES INC
HSY	Industrial	NYSE	HERSHEY FOODS CORP
HWP	Industrial	NYSE	HEWLETT PACKARD CO
HLT	Industrial	NYSE	HILTON HOTELS CORP
HD	Industrial	NYSE	HOME DEPOT INC
HM	Industrial	NYSE	HOMESTAKE MINING CO
HON	Industrial	NYSE	HONEYWELL INC
HI	Financial	NYSE	HOUSEHOLD INTL INC
HOU	Utilities	NYSE	HOUSTON INDUSTRIES INC
HUM	Industrial	NYSE	HUMANA INC
HBAN	Financial	NASD	HUNTINGTON BANCSHARES
IKN	Industrial	NYSE	IKON OFFICE SOLUTIONS
ITW	Industrial	NYSE	ILLINOIS TOOL WORKS INC
RX	Industrial	NYSE	IMS HEALTH INC
N	Industrial	NYSE	INCO LTD
IR	Industrial	NYSE	INGERSOLL RAND CO
INTC	Industrial	NASD	INTEL CORP
IBM	Industrial	NYSE	INTERNATIONAL BUSINESS MACHINES
IFF	Industrial	NYSE	INTERNATIONAL FLAV & FRAG

Symbol	S&P Group	Exchange	Issue Name
IP	Industrial	NYSE	INTERNATIONAL PAPER CO
IPG	Industrial	NYSE	INTERPUBLIC GROUP COS INC
IIN	Industrial	NYSE	ITT INDUSTRIES INC
JP	Financial	NYSE	JEFFERSON PILOT CORP
JNJ	Industrial	NYSE	JOHNSON & JOHNSON
JCI	Industrial	NYSE	JOHNSON CONTROLS INC
JOS	Industrial	NYSE	JOSTENS INC
KM	Industrial	NYSE	K MART CORP
KBH	Industrial	NYSE	KAUFMAN & BROAD HOME CORP
K	Industrial	NYSE	KELLOGG CO
KMG	Industrial	NYSE	KERR MCGEE CORP
KEY	Financial	NYSE	KEYCORP
KMB	Industrial	NYSE	KIMBERLY CLARK CORP
KWP	Industrial	NYSE	KING WORLD PRODS INC
KLAC	Industrial	NASD	KLA-TENCOR CORP
KRI	Industrial	NYSE	KNIGHT RIDDER INC
KSS	Industrial	NYSE	KOHL'S CORP
KR	Industrial	NYSE	KROGER CO
LDW	Industrial	NYSE	LAIDLAW INC
LEH	Financial	NYSE	LEHMAN BROS HLDGS
LLY	Industrial	NYSE	LILLY ELI & CO
LTD	Industrial	NYSE	LIMITED INC
LNC	Financial	NYSE	LINCOLN NATIONAL CORP
LIZ	Industrial	NYSE	LIZ CLAIBORNE INC
LMT	Industrial	NYSE	LOCKHEED MARTIN CORP
LTR	Financial	NYSE	LOEWS CORP
LDG	Industrial	NYSE	LONGS DRUG STORES CORP
LPX	Industrial	NYSE	LOUISIANA PACIFIC CORP
LOW	Industrial	NYSE	LOWES COS INC
LSI	Industrial	NYSE	LSI LOGIC CORP
LU	Industrial	NYSE	LUCENT TECHNOLOGIES

Symbol	S&P Group	Exchange	Issue Name
MKG	Industrial	NYSE	MALLINCKRODT GROUP INC
MAR	Industrial	NYSE	MARRIOTT INTL INC
MMC	Financial	NYSE	MARSH & MCLENNAN
MAS	Industrial	NYSE	MASCO CORP
MAT	Industrial	NYSE	MATTEL INC
MAY	Industrial	NYSE	MAY DEPT STORES CO
MYG	Industrial	NYSE	MAYTAG CORP
MBI	Financial	NYSE	MBIA INC
KRB	Financial	NYSE	MBNA CORP
MDR	Industrial	NYSE	MCDERMOTT INTL INC
MCD	Industrial	NYSE	MCDONALDS CORP
MHP	Industrial	NYSE	MCGRAW HILL COS INC
WCOM	Industrial	NASD	MCI WORLDCOM
MEA	Industrial	NYSE	MEAD CORP
UMG	Industrial	NYSE	MEDIAONE GROUP INC
MDT	Industrial	NYSE	MEDTRONIC INC
MEL	Financial	NYSE	MELLON BANK CORP
MTL	Financial	NYSE	MERCANTILE BANCORP
MRK	Industrial	NYSE	MERCK & CO INC
MDP	Industrial	NYSE	MEREDITH CORP
MER	Financial	NYSE	MERRILL LYNCH & CO INC
FMY	Industrial	NYSE	MEYER (FRED) INC
MTG	Financial	NYSE	MGIC INVESTMENT
MU	Industrial	NYSE	MICRON TECHNOLOGY INC
MSFT	Industrial	NASD	MICROSOFT CORP
MZ	Industrial	NYSE	MILACRON INC
MIL	Industrial	NYSE	MILLIPORE CORP
MMM	Industrial	NYSE	MINNESOTA MNG & MFG CO
MIR	Industrial	NYSE	MIRAGE RESORTS
MOB	Industrial	NYSE	MOBIL CORP
MTC	Industrial	NYSE	MONSANTO CO
MCL	Industrial	NYSE	MOORE CORP LTD
JPM	Financial	NYSE	MORGAN J P & CO INC
MWD	Financial	NYSE	MORGAN STANLEY, DEAN WITTER & CO
MII	Industrial	NYSE	MORTON INTL INC IND

Symbol	S&P Group	Exchange	Issue Name
MOT	Industrial	NYSE	MOTOROLA INC
NC	Industrial	NYSE	NACCO INDUSTRIES INC
NLC	Industrial	NYSE	NALCO CHEMICAL CO
NCC	Financial	NYSE	NATIONAL CITY CORP
NSM	Industrial	NYSE	NATIONAL SEMICONDUCTOR CO
NSI	Industrial	NYSE	NATIONAL SERVICE INDS INC
NAV	Industrial	NYSE	NAVISTAR INTL CORP
NCE	Utilities	NYSE	NEW CENTURY ENERGIES
NYT	Industrial	NYSE	NEW YORK TIMES CL A
NWL	Industrial	NYSE	NEWELL CO
NEM	Industrial	NYSE	NEWMONT MINING CORP
NXTL	Industrial	NASD	NEXTEL COMMUNICATIONS
NMK	Utilities	NYSE	NIAGARA MOHAWK POWER CORP
GAS	Utilities	NYSE	NICOR INC
NKE	Industrial	NYSE	NIKE INC CL B
NOBE	Industrial	NASD	NORDSTROM INC
NSC	Transportation	NYSE	NORFOLK SOUTHERN CORP
NSP	Utilities	NYSE	NORTHERN STES PWR CO MN
NT	Industrial	NYSE	NORTHERN TELECOM LTD
NTRS	Financial	NASD	NORTHERN TRUST CORP
NOC	Industrial	NYSE	NORTHROP GRUMMAN CORP
NOVL	Industrial	NASD	NOVELL INC
NUE	Industrial	NYSE	NUCOR CORP
OXY	Industrial	NYSE	OCCIDENTAL PETROLEUM CORP
OMC	Industrial	NYSE	OMNICOM GROUP
OKE	Utilities	NYSE	ONEOK INC
ORCL	Industrial	NASD	ORACLE CORP
ORX	Industrial	NYSE	ORYX ENERGY CO
OWC	Industrial	NYSE	OWENS CORNING

Symbol	*S&P Group*	*Exchange*	*Issue Name*
OI	Industrial	NYSE	OWENS-ILLINOIS
PCAR	Industrial	NASD	PACCAR INC
PPW	Utilities	NYSE	PACIFICORP
PLL	Industrial	NYSE	PALL CORP
PMTC	Industrial	NASD	PARAMETRIC TECHNOLOGY
PH	Industrial	NYSE	PARKER HANNIFIN CORP
PAYX	Industrial	NASD	PAYCHEX INC
PE	Utilities	NYSE	PECO ENERGY CO
JCP	Industrial	NYSE	PENNEY J C CO INC
PGL	Utilities	NYSE	PEOPLES ENERGY CORP
PSFT	Industrial	NASD	PEOPLESOFT INC
PBY	Industrial	NYSE	PEP BOYS MANNY MOE & JACK
PEP	Industrial	NYSE	PEPSICO INC
PKN	Industrial	NYSE	PERKIN ELMER CORP
PFE	Industrial	NYSE	PFIZER INC
PCG	Utilities	NYSE	PG&E CORP
PNU	Industrial	NYSE	PHARMACIA & UPJOHN INC
PD	Industrial	NYSE	PHELPS DODGE CORP
MO	Industrial	NYSE	PHILIP MORRIS COS INC
P	Industrial	NYSE	PHILLIPS PETROLEUM CO
PHB	Industrial	NASD	PIONEER HI BRED INTL INC
PBI	Industrial	NYSE	PITNEY BOWES INC
PDG	Industrial	NYSE	PLACER DOME INC
PNC	Financial	NYSE	PNC BANK CORP
PRD	Industrial	NYSE	POLAROID CORP
PCH	Industrial	NYSE	POTLATCH CORP
PPL	Utilities	NYSE	PP & L RESOURCES INC
PPG	Industrial	NYSE	PPG INDUSTRIES INC
PX	Industrial	NYSE	PRAXAIR INC
PG	Industrial	NYSE	PROCTER & GAMBLE CO
PGR	Financial	NYSE	PROGRESSIVE CORP
PVT	Financial	NYSE	PROVIDENT COMPANIES INC
PVN	Financial	NYSE	PROVIDIAN CORP
PEG	Utilities	NYSE	PUBLIC SERVICE ENTPR GRP

Symbol	S&P Group	Exchange	Issue Name
PHM	Industrial	NYSE	PULTE CORP
OAT	Industrial	NYSE	QUAKER OATS CO
RAL	Industrial	NYSE	RALSTON-RALSTN PURINA GRP
RYC	Industrial	NYSE	RAYCHEM CORP
RTN/B	Industrial	NYSE	RAYTHEON CO
RBK	Industrial	NYSE	REEBOK INTL LTD
RGBK	Financial	NASD	REGIONS FINANCIAL CORP
RNB	Financial	NYSE	REPUBLIC NEW YORK
RLM	Industrial	NYSE	REYNOLDS METALS CO
RAD	Industrial	NYSE	RITE AID CORP
RN	Industrial	NYSE	RJR NABISCO HOLDINGS CORP
ROK	Industrial	NYSE	ROCKWELL INTL CORP
ROH	Industrial	NYSE	ROHM & HAAS CO
RDC	Industrial	NYSE	ROWAN COS INC
RD	Industrial	NYSE	ROYAL DUTCH PETROLEUM CO
RBD	Industrial	NYSE	RUBBERMAID INC
RML	Industrial	NYSE	RUSSELL CORP
R	Transportation	NYSE	RYDER SYSTEM INC
SAFC	Financial	NASD	SAFECO CORP
SWY	Industrial	NYSE	SAFEWAY INC
SLE	Industrial	NYSE	SARA LEE CORP
SBC	Utilities	NYSE	SBC COMMUNICATIONS INC
SGP	Industrial	NYSE	SCHERING-PLOUGH
SLB	Industrial	NYSE	SCHLUMBERGER LTD
SFA	Industrial	NYSE	SCIENTIFIC ATLANTA INC
SEG	Industrial	NYSE	SEAGATE TECHNOLOGY
VO	Industrial	NYSE	SEAGRAM CO LTD
SEE	Industrial	NYSE	SEALED AIR CORP
S	Industrial	NYSE	SEARS ROEBUCK & CO
SRE	Utilities	NYSE	SEMPRA ENERGY
SRV	Industrial	NYSE	SERVICE CORP INTL
SMS	Industrial	NASD	SHARED MEDICAL SYS CORP
SHW	Industrial	NYSE	SHERWIN WILLIAMS CO
SIAL	Industrial	NASD	SIGMA ALDRICH CORP

Symbol	S&P Group	Exchange	Issue Name
SGI	Industrial	NYSE	SILICON GRAPHICS INC
SLM	Financial	NYSE	SLM HOLDING CORP
SNA	Industrial	NYSE	SNAP ON INC HOLDING CO
SLR	Industrial	NYSE	SOLECTRON
SNT	Utilities	NYSE	SONAT INC
SO	Utilities	NYSE	SOUTHERN CO
LUV	Transportation	NYSE	SOUTHWEST AIRLINES CO
SMI	Industrial	NYSE	SPRINGS INDUSTRIES INC
FON	Industrial	NYSE	SPRINT CORP FON GROUP
PCS	Industrial	NYSE	SPRINT CORP PCS GROUP
STJ	Industrial	NASD	ST JUDE MEDICAL INC
SPC	Financial	NYSE	ST PAUL COS INC
SWK	Industrial	NYSE	STANLEY WORKS
SPLS	Industrial	NASD	STAPLES INC
STT	Financial	NYSE	STATE STREET CORP
SUB	Financial	NYSE	SUMMIT BANCORP
SUNW	Industrial	NASD	SUN MICROSYSTEMS INC
SUN	Industrial	NYSE	SUNOCO INC
STI	Financial	NYSE	SUNTRUST BANKS
SVU	Industrial	NYSE	SUPERVALU INC
SNV	Financial	NYSE	SYNOVUS FINANCIAL
SYY	Industrial	NYSE	SYSCO CORP
TAN	Industrial	NYSE	TANDY CORP
TEK	Industrial	NYSE	TEKTRONIX INC
TCOMA	Industrial	NASD	TELE-COMMUNICATIONS
TLAB	Industrial	NASD	TELLABS INC
TIN	Industrial	NYSE	TEMPLE INLAND INC
THC	Industrial	NYSE	TENET HEALTHCARE CORP
TEN	Industrial	NYSE	TENNECO INC HLDG CO
TX	Industrial	NYSE	TEXACO INC
TXN	Industrial	NYSE	TEXAS INSTRUMENTS INC
TXU	Utilities	NYSE	TEXAS UTILITIES CO
TXT	Industrial	NYSE	TEXTRON INC
TMO	Industrial	NYSE	THERMO ELECTRON

Symbol	S&P Group	Exchange	Issue Name
TNB	Industrial	NYSE	THOMAS & BETTS CORP
TWX	Industrial	NYSE	TIME WARNER INC
TMC	Industrial	NYSE	TIMES MIRROR CO
TKR	Industrial	NYSE	TIMKEN CO
TJX	Industrial	NYSE	TJX COMPANIES INC
TMK	Financial	NYSE	TORCHMARK CORP
TOY	Industrial	NYSE	TOYS R US INC
TA	Financial	NYSE	TRANSAMERICA CORP
TRB	Industrial	NYSE	TRIBUNE CO
YUM	Industrial	NYSE	TRICON GLOBAL RESTAURANTS
TRW	Industrial	NYSE	TRW INC
TUP	Industrial	NYSE	TUPPERWARE CORP
TYC	Industrial	NYSE	TYCO INTERNATIONAL LTD
USB	Financial	NASD	U.S. BANCORP
UCM	Utilities	NYSE	UNICOM CORP HOLDING CO
UN	Industrial	NYSE	UNILEVER N V
UCC	Industrial	NYSE	UNION CAMP CORP
UK	Industrial	NYSE	UNION CARBIDE CORP
UNP	Transportation	NYSE	UNION PACIFIC
UPR	Industrial	NYSE	UNION PACIFIC RESOURCES GROUP
UPC	Financial	NYSE	UNION PLANTERS
UIS	Industrial	NYSE	UNISYS CORP
UNH	Industrial	NYSE	UNITED HEALTHCARE CORP
UTX	Industrial	NYSE	UNITED TECHNOLOGIES CORP
UCL	Industrial	NYSE	UNOCAL CORP
UNM	Financial	NYSE	UNUM CORP
USW	Utilities	NYSE	US WEST INC
U	Transportation	NYSE	USAIR GROUP INC
UST	Industrial	NYSE	UST INC
MRO	Industrial	NYSE	USX-MARATHON GROUP
X	Industrial	NYSE	USX-U.S. STEEL GROUP
VFC	Industrial	NYSE	V F CORP
VIA/B	Industrial	AMEX	VIACOM INC
WB	Financial	NYSE	WACHOVIA CORP

Symbol	*S&P Group*	*Exchange*	*Issue Name*
WMT	Industrial	NYSE	WAL MART STORES INC
WAG	Industrial	NYSE	WALGREEN CO
DIS	Industrial	NYSE	WALT DISNEY CO
WLA	Industrial	NYSE	WARNER LAMBERT CO
WM	Financial	NYSE	WASHINGTON MUTUAL INC
WMI	Industrial	NYSE	WASTE MANAGEMENT
WFC	Financial	NYSE	WELLS FARGO & CO
WEN	Industrial	NYSE	WENDYS INTERNATIONAL INC
W	Industrial	NYSE	WESTVACO CORP
WY	Industrial	NYSE	WEYERHAEUSER CO
WHR	Industrial	NYSE	WHIRLPOOL CORP
WLL	Industrial	NYSE	WILLAMETTE INDUSTRIES
WMB	Utilities	NYSE	WILLIAMS COS
WIN	Industrial	NYSE	WINN DIXIE STORES INC
WTHG	Industrial	NASD	WORTHINGTON INDS INC
WWY	Industrial	NYSE	WRIGLEY WM JR CO
XRX	Industrial	NYSE	XEROX CORP

Appendix B

Excerpts from the TradeCast 3.0 User Manual

Welcome

Welcome to the TradeCast version 3.0 help guide. This help guide has been designed to meet several needs.

Primarily this guide strives to be a tool for maximizing your use of TradeCast version 3.0 and all of its features. This latest version of Trader Pro has a great deal more features than ever before, but prior to using them for your trading it will be extremely beneficial to you to take the time to learn them fully.

We've broken this guide down by individual windows inside of version 3.0 to better facilitate you when you're searching for specifics about a particular window or function.

We hope you find the guide informative and helpful. If you have any suggestions on how to improve this guide, whether it is the addition of an untouched subject or simply a clarification, please email us at documentation@tcast.com and we'll try to work it in.

Thanks,
The TradeCast Technical Support Team

What is TradeCast Trader?

- Version 3.0 is the latest release of TradeCast client software for trading securities listed on the NASDAQ, NYSE, AMEX markets and ECN's such as the ISLAND ECN.
- Version 3.0 lets you make a trade for yourself in seconds at your desired price. This is in direct contrast to calling a brokerage and placing an order that may be filled in several minutes or several hours—at a price that may or may not reflect where the market was when you placed your order.
- Version 3.0 provides full access to trade NASDAQ stocks via SOES, Select Net, as well as to the New York Stock Exchange and AMEX. It also allows direct access to the ISLAND ECN as well as all other ECN's via Select Net. Other ECN access is soon to follow.
- Version 3.0 also allows you to take advantage of the best quotes and fastest executions offered by a software developer today.
- TradeCast version 3.0 allows you to choose the method with which you use the program—mouse or keyboard. We realize that some traders enjoy the ease of use that accompanies using the mouse as a primary input device and that some traders enjoy the speed and flexibility of the keyboard and programmable keystrokes.

What's New

- Several exciting new features have been introduced with version 3.0:
- Complete customization of the following:
  - Stock window
  - Ticker window
  - Indices
  - New High Low
  - Filters
  - Blotter window
- Programmable keystrokes
  - OTC (Over the Counter)
  - Listed (NYSE & AMEX)
- Real-time profit and loss window
- Faster quotes delivery platform
- New exchange defaults
- Integrated ISLAND Book

- Pre-made layouts and window templates
- Customizable Board Views
- New print window feature
- New Top 10 windows
- Fundamental Data
- Company Names
- Improved Trade Basket interface and functionality
- Indices window
- Powerful new linking features
- Clock Display

Table of Contents:

I. Minimum Requirements

TradeCast version 3.0 is the most advanced product we've ever offered. To get the most out of its many advanced features, you'll want to make sure that your computer fits the following minimum requirements. While you might be tempted to run version 3.0 on lower systems, you're sacrificing speed that could give you an added advantage over other traders using less sophisticated software.

- Intel Pentium 133 MHz
- 512K Level II cache
- 32 MB RAM
- Video card capable of *at least* 1024×768 resolution with a 16-bit color palette

- Note: The higher the resolution your video card is capable of translates directly into how much screen "real estate" you'll have for charts, tickers, board views, and other windows.
- Windows®95 OSR 2 Windows®98
- 1 GB hard drive (at least 200 MB free space)

For our in-house brokerage users/LAN Users

10/100 Network Interface Card (NIC) TradeCast strongly recommends a 3Com 905TX NIC. They may be purchased in many retail establishments as well as from any reputable hardware reseller.

For our Internet users

Internet access through an Internet Service Provider. Online services such as America Online (AOL) are unacceptable and will hamper version 3.0's performance greatly. TradeCast recommends a provider that directly interfaces with the MCI WorldCom, UUNet, PSI Net, or Cable & Wireless all have direct connections to the TradeCast Internet Quote Servers.

Other recommendations

TradeCast firmly believes that you should treat your computer, whether it is on a Local Area Network (LAN), at a brokerage firm, or at home in your office as a *dedicated trading workstation.* TradeCast recommends that no additional software be installed on the system. If you bought your computer new, TradeCast highly suggests removing ALL unnecessary software installed by the manufacturer at the very least if not reformatting the hard drive and installing nothing but the operating system and version 3.0. Also, make sure no extraneous network protocols are installed. Set a permanent swap file via Windows' virtual memory settings, and de-fragment your hard drive regularly.

We do understand that you may depend on other software for information that is mission critical to your individual style of trading. If possible, please install it on a secondary machine. If there is no other viable alternative and you do install additional software on your TradeCast workstation, please be aware that it may not function correctly or could interfere with version 3.0's operation.

4. Accessing and Customizing the Trading Tools

The individual trading Tools are located within the Tools menu.

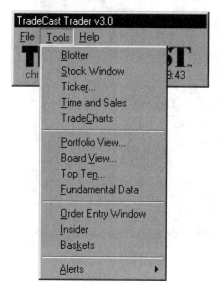

Blotter

To Open the Blotter, go to the Tools, pull-down menu and select Blotter. The Blotter window is comprised of three panes—Open Positions, Summary, and Trades. To switch among the three tabs, simply click on the labeled tabs towards the top of the window.

Blotter: CMOORE					☒

Open Positions		Summary		Trades	

Symbol	Side	Shares	Cost	P/L	Trade Time
EBAY	B	1000	160.50	22,562.50	14:43:00
INTC	B	1000	114.56	1,625.00	11:49:00
WCOM	B	1000	60.94	812.50	11:57:00

Open Positions Tab

The Open Positions Tab of the Blotter allows you to keep track of any open positions you are currently holding. It is completely customizable and allows you to mix and match 25 different pieces of information and then display that information in the format that best fits your trading style.

Open summary will show weighted average price instead of the average price. For example:

Suppose you had the following open positions:

BOT	MSFT	126	1000 Shares
BOT	MSFT	126 1/8	500 Shares

The old version would show:	BOT	MSFT	126.0625	1500 Shares
The new version	BOT	MSFT	126.0416	1500 Shares

Summary Tab

The Summary Tab contains information about the progress and results of your trading for the current day such as equity, margin, P/L, and number of trades.

It is important to understand that not all fields on the Summary Tab are updated in real-time. Some of the fields are only updated by clicking the Open Positions Tab or Trades Tab and then clicking back to the Summary Tab.

Real-time Fields

Open Positions: Your current number of open positions.

Open Trades: Your current number of open trades.

Exposure Long: The amount of your margin used by open long positions.

Exposure Short: The amount of your margin used by open short positions.

Total Exposure: The amount of your margin used by both long and short open positions.

Refreshable Fields

Trades Today: Total number of trades executed during the current day.

Current Margin: The amount of margin available to your account.

Realized Profit and Loss: The amount of money your account has gained or lost on all trades that have been both opened and closed. Note that this does not include any commissions, market charges, ECN charges, or other miscellaneous charges associated with trading via your brokerage.

Unrealized Profit and Loss: The amount of money your account would gain or lose on closing all open trades via buy or sell orders executed at the inside bid or ask. Note that this does not include any commissions, market charges, ECN charges, or other miscellaneous charges associated with trading via your brokerage.

Startup Equity: The amount of equity contained in your account at the beginning of the current day.

Current Equity: The difference between your Startup Equity and the current bid price.

Long Shares: Current number of shares long in your open positions.

Short Shares: Current number of shares short in your open positions.

Total Shares: Current number of shares both short and long in your open positions.

Trades Tab

The Trades Tab allows to you to review *all* of your trades for a given day in addition to viewing your open positions. The Trades Tab contains the following columns, listed below as they appear from right to left:

```
Blotter: CMOORE                                    [x]
  Open Positions  |  Summary   |   Trades      |
    View Option: [Open Trades      ▼] Sort Option: [Stock ▼]
  EWBX B 48 3/4   1000 ISLD 13:49:00 ACTS 0.0  327 327
  TGLO B 36 1/2   1000 ISLD 13:52:00 ACTS 0.0  328 328
```

Stock Symbol, Side of Trade (buy, sell, or short sell), Price of Execution, Number of Shares, Time of Execution, Market of Execution (SOES, EEXO, or ISLD), Profit or Loss on Trade (only appears on closing trades)

Refreshing the Trades Tab

The Trades Tab is not real-time. Trades executed after the most recent time will not appear until the Trades Tab is refreshed. The Trades Tab may be refreshed in either of two ways. You can right-click on the large white window where information is displayed on the Trades Tab and left-click once on "Refresh" from the menu that appears. You may also refresh the Trades Tab by clicking on the Open Positions Tab or the Summary Tab and then clicking back to the Trades Tab.

Display Options

The Trades Tab contains two view adjustable options that allow you to view your trade information in the manner you find most useful. They are the View Option and the Sort Option.

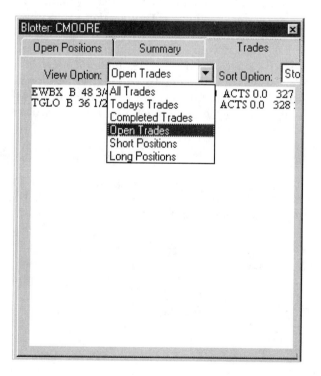

View

This option allows you to look at: All Trades, Today's Trades, Completed Trades, Open Trades, Short Positions, Long Positions.

You can also access your account information by pressing on the Summary Tab. Every time you switch from Trades to Summary, new information is brought to your display. Please realize the information displayed here is based on data provided by the brokerage firm you trade at. They will be able to assist you with any inconsistencies.

We have made some changes to the blotter window to increase the speed of the overall program and to prevent the program from "locking up" in case of a SQL Server crash.

Past versions of Trader Pro required you to refresh your blotter by clicking back and forth between tabs, sometimes making it difficult to keep track of positions resulting or affected by orders filled on other systems such as Instinet. Version 3.0 corrects this problem—as soon as the brokerage employee enters the transaction into Manual Order Entry it will be displayed on the version 3.0 blotter.

You can switch between the different View Options by clicking on the downward triangle directly to the right of the file displaying the current selected View Option, highlighting the View Option you wish to display, then releasing the left-mouse button.

The Sort Option lets you sort your trades by either Stock (symbols in alphabetical order) or Time (Ascending or Descending Order). You can switch between the two Sort Options by clicking on the downward triangle directly to the right of the file displaying the current selected Sort option, highlighting the Sort Option you wish to display, then releasing the left-mouse button.

Appearance changes

To access the menu for appearance changes, right mouse click in the data area of the Open Positions Tab of your blotter. This will allow you to access templates, customize, refresh and print.

Templates

The template section is available for a pre-configured blotter design.

Customization

To customize your blotter right mouse click on the Open Positions Tab of your blotter and then left-clicking on "Customize".

The 4 customization sections

The Blotter's customization window is sub-divided into four sections: columns, options, font, and colors. To switch amongst them, simply click on the labeled tabs towards the top of the window.

The Columns Tab

Your blotter's Open Positions Tab is capable of displaying as many as 25 fields, each one containing different information about every one of your open positions. There's a good likelihood you may only want to see a handful of these fields displayed at one time.

```
Blotter Customization                                    [x]

 Columns | Options | Font | Colors |

 ┌────────────────┐        ┌────────────────┐
 │ Ask         ▲  │        │ Symbol         │
 │ Bid            │   ┌──┐ │ Side           │  ┌──┐
 │ Close          │   │ >│ │ Shares         │  │ ^│
 │ High           │   └──┘ │ Cost           │  └──┘
 │ Last           │        │ P/L            │
 │ Time           │   ┌──┐ │ Trade Time     │  ┌──┐
 │ Low            │   │ <│ │                │  │ v│
 │ Change         │   └──┘ └────────────────┘  └──┘
 │ Open           │
 │ Size           │   ┌─ Column Settings ──────────┐
 │ Volume         │   │                            │
 │ PB High        │   │  Width (in chars) [      ] │
 │ PB Low         │   │                            │
 │ Name        ▼  │   │  Alignment      [      ▼]  │
 └────────────────┘   └────────────────────────────┘

 ┌──────────┐    ┌──────────┐    ┌──────────┐
 │   Ok     │    │  Cancel  │    │  Apply   │
 └──────────┘    └──────────┘    └──────────┘

 ┌──────────────┐    ┌──────────────────┐
 │ Load Default │    │ Save as Default  │
 └──────────────┘    └──────────────────┘
```

Stock Window

To Open the Stock Window, go to the Tools located on the Trader Bar and click on Tools to access the Stock Window.

Viewing Quotes in the Stock Window

To view a quote, type the symbol in the symbol field at the upper left-hand corner of the Stock Window and press Enter. The full company name for the stock symbol will be displayed in the title bar of the Stock Window and the window itself will display a great deal of Level I and Level II data.

Information Displayed in the Stock Window

The Stock Window displays all manners of Level I and Level II information. In addition to being highly customizable it serves as the vehicle for many of version 3.0's order entry functions.

Appearance changes

To access the menu for appearance changes, right mouse click in the data area of the colored Market Maker section. This will allow you to access 'clear load', 'clear buttons', 'view load section', 'uppercase symbols', 'templates', 'customize', 'refresh' and 'print'.

Clear Load

Pressing this button clears all inputted information, and returns all fields to initial defaults in the load section.

Clear Buttons

Use this when you want to further extend a position. I.E., six minutes ago, you opened an INTC long position and now wish to purchase additional shares rather than selling the position.

View Load Section

Experienced TradeCast users will disable the load section and use the order entry keystrokes for executions. This allows them to have more real estate on their desktop.

View Load Section   View Load Section (unchecked)

Templates

The template section is available for a pre-configured stock window design.

Customize

The Stock Window's Customization Section is sub-divided into four Tabs: Columns, Options, Font and Colors. To switch among them, simply click on the labeled tabs towards the top of the window. To access this customization section, right mouse click in the colored (Level II) section of the Stock window. This will not send an order.

Columns Tab

Your stock window is capable of displaying as many as 8 fields, each one containing different information about every one of the Market Makers within the Level II window.

Tickers

Open ticker

To open a ticker, go to the Tools pull-down menu and select Ticker. This will open the Launch New Ticker window pictured below.

After opening the Launch New Ticker window, you will first need to select the style of ticker you wish to launch. To change between the different styles of tickers, click the downward triangle at the top right of the Launch New Ticker Window, scroll through the various options, highlight the desired style, and release the left mouse button.

Next, highlight the name of the ticker you wish to launch. TradeCast includes many tickers within version 3.0 that allow you to track specific indexes and entire industries. You may also create your own custom ticker. Then check/uncheck the ticker settings so that the ticker will only display information you wish to view. Finally, click the Launch button to exit the Launch New Ticker window and start the ticker.

NOTE: The above instructions apply only to launching a pre-existing ticker. Creating a new ticker from scratch is discussed later in this manual.

Setting Ticker Parameters

The bottom section of the Launch New Ticker window contains four check boxes that comprise the ticker settings. Before launching any ticker, you will need to check the boxes corresponding to the information you wish the ticker to display.

High/Low: The High/Low checkbox is unique amongst the ticker settings in that once it is checked, the remaining three checkboxes become inaccessible—if you choose to display High/Low information in a ticker you will need additional tickers to display other information for the same list of stocks. The High/Low ticker shows both new daily highs and lows as well as counts the numbers of highs and lows. This allows you to take notice of each individual stock in your ticker that is consistently reaching new highs or lows. You're much more apt to take a look at a stock that has hit its tenth daily high in the last two minutes then a stock hitting its second daily low in the same time period. The High/Low ticker also displays a stock's net gain or loss since the open.

Trades:　Checking the Trades box allows your ticker to display the same information contained in a Time of Sales window.

Level 1:　Checking the Level 1 box allows your ticker to display any changes to the Inside Bid or Ask.

Level 2:　Checking the Level 2 box allows your ticker to display all quotation changes by any Market Maker or ECN.

Adding and removing symbols from Tickers

To add or remove a symbol from any existing ticker other then a 'quick' or open positions ticker you must first access the ticker symbol list by either right-clicking on the ticker and selecting 'Edit List'.

The ticker symbol list displays all stocks currently in your ticker on the far right side of the window. To remove a single symbol, click on it once to highlight it and then click the Delete button on the left side of the window. If for whatever reason you would like to remove all the symbols currently being displayed by your ticker simply click the Delete All button once. To add a symbol to your ticker, type the symbol in the small field at the top left of the window and either press the Enter button on your keyboard or click the Add button once with your mouse. When you have finished adding and removing symbols from your ticker, click the Close button to close the ticker symbol list.

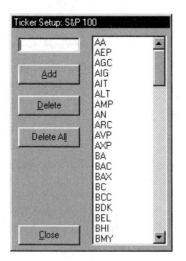

Ticker Styles

There are three different ticker types that are available in version 3.0: Positions Tickers, Quick Tickers, and Custom Tickers.

Positions Ticker

Positions Tickers keep you updated on price changes and trades in securities in which you hold an open position.

Long Positions Ticker: This ticker will display information only for securities in which you are currently long. Stocks are added and removed from this ticker automatically.

Short Positions Ticker: This ticker will display information only for securities in which you are currently short. Stocks are added and removed from this ticker automatically.

Open Positions Ticker: This ticker will display information only for securities in which you are currently open, whether it is long or short. Stocks are added and removed from this ticker automatically.

Quick Tickers

Quick Tickers allow you to add or remove a stock from directly within a Stock window without having to edit a ticker stock list. To add a stock to a Quick ticker, simply hold down the ALT and press the T on the keyboard while the focus is on the Stock window displaying the security you wish to view in your ticker. To remove the stock, hold down the ALT and press D on the keyboard while the focus is on the stock window displaying the stock in which you wish to remove from your ticker.

Custom Tickers

Custom Tickers display only stocks that the trader specifies for the ticker. Stocks may not be added or removed in the same manner as they are with the Quick Ticker, but can display as few or as many symbols as the trader desires.

Creating a New Ticker

To open a ticker, go to the Tools pull-down menu and select Ticker. This will open the launch new ticker window. Under style, select custom and then click the 'New' button once, bringing up the new ticker dialogue box. Type the name you wish to assign to the ticker and press Enter on the keyboard or click the OK button. This will bring up the ticker symbol list. Add the symbols you wish to appear in your custom ticker as described previously. When you are finished editing the list of symbols click the Close button and launch your ticker.

Time of Sales Window

To open a Time of Sales window, go to the Tools pull-down menu and select Time and Sales. This will open a Time of Sales window such as the one pictured below.

```
INTC                              ×
┌────────────────────┐
│                    │
├────────────────────┤
14:27    101  1/16      200  Q     ▲
14:27    101  1/8       400  Q     
14:27    101  1/8       500  Q     
14:27  a 101  1/8        30  Q     
14:27  b 101  1/16        5  Q     
14:27  a 101  1/8        30  Q     
14:27  b 101  1/16       10  Q     
14:27    101  1/8       300  Q     
14:27  a 101  1/8        30  Q  U  
14:27  b 101  1/16       10  Q  U  
14:27    101  1/16      100  Q     
14:27    101  1/16      100  Q     
14:27  a 101  1/8        30  Q     
14:27  b 101           10  Q     
14:27    101         30000  Q     
14:27    101  1/16     3500  Q     
14:26    101  3/32     1000  Q     
14:26  a 101  1/16       30  Q     
14:26  b 101           10  Q     
14:26    101  1/16      200  Q     
14:26    100  5/16      200  Q  X  ▼
```

The above Time of Sale window displays the following real time:

- Time of sale: The actual time the
- Bid/ask:
- Price of sale:
- Shares amount:
- Market: Q = NASDAQ NMS, S = NASDAQ Small Cap, N = New York Stock Exchange, A = American Stock Exchange, B = Boston Stock Exchange, M = Midwest Stock Exchange, T = Philadelphia Stock Exchange, X = Cincinnati Stock Exchange, P = Pacific Stock Exchange.
- Messaging: A = acquisition, B= bunched trade, C= cash sale, D = distribution, G= bunched sold trade, K= rule 155 trade, L= sold last, N= next day, O= opened, R= seller, S= split trade, T= form T (pre/post MKT hours), W= average price trade, X= cancelled, Z= out of sequence

Color settings

By Right mouse clicking in the Time of Sales window, you can access changes in Fonts as well as changes in the 'BID', 'ASK' and 'Quote' Color. Changes made to a Time of Sale window will only affect that particular Time of Sale window.

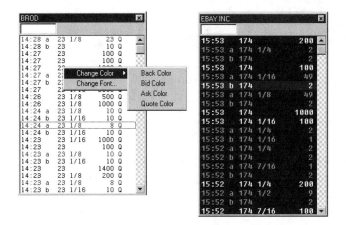

Portfolio View

To open a portfolio view, go to the Tools pull-down menu and select Portfolio view. This will open the Portfolio Launch window as pictured below.

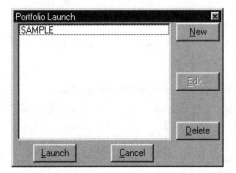

Highlight the name of the portfolio you wish to view and then click the Launch button. This will open up the Portfolio.

Portfolio - SAMPLE					☒
Unrealized P/L [4,343.75]					
Symbol	Side	Shares	Cost	P/L	Trade Time
ADVH	B	400	12.56	(4,375.00)	15:48:26
ESCI	B	600	1.00	(187.50)	15:48:26
ISWI	B	500	1.25	218.75	15:48:26
PQT	B	300	1.88	0.00	15:48:26
SMU	B	100	10.00	0.00	15:48:26

Information Displayed in the Portfolio View

The Portfolio can be considered almost a second blotter—it, however, is meant for any long-term positions your account may be holding or perhaps even all of your holdings from another account not specifically used for active trading. The Portfolio is capable of being customized in the same manner as the Blotter. Just like the Blotter, you will need to choose which of the available fields you wish for your Portfolio to display. Also like the Blotter, you can set which fields are displayed in the Portfolio by right clicking on the Portfolio and choosing Customize. This will open the Portfolio Customization window that functions exactly as the Blotter Customization window. Another method in which to change which fields are displayed on the Portfolio is to right-click on the Portfolio and choose Change Portfolio. This will open the Portfolio Change window, which looks and functions exactly as the Portfolio Launch window does. From here you may select another style of Portfolio by highlighting its name and clicking the OK button.

Adding and Removing Positions from the Portfolio View

When you first open a Portfolio, it will be blank and you will need to input any open positions you would like it to track. Right click on the Portfolio and choose Edit Position. This will launch the Portfolio Trade Input window. First, enter the symbol in the symbol field. As you enter the symbol various company names will be displayed to the right of the field as Trader matches symbols to company names. When you have completed typing in the symbol you should see the correct full name of the company displayed to the right of the Symbol field. Next, enter the number of shares of stock that you have in the position in the Shares field. After entering the number of shares you will need to add the price that the trade was executed at. You can enter the price in either decimal format or in a fraction format. For example, assume that the price of execution was $47^{15}/_{16}$. You could either add the price as "$47^{15}/_{16}$" or as "47.9375", whichever is most convenient for you. Finally, you will need to specify the Side of the trade that you are currently open. Click the downward pointing triangle to the right of the Side field and select Buy, Sell, or Short Sell. When you have finished completing all fields totally and completely, click the Ok button to return to your Portfolio. The position you entered should appear and any fields that you have selected to display containing real-time information should update automatically.

Board Views

To open a Board View window, go to the Tools pull-down menu and select Board View . . . This will open the Board View Launch window such as the one pictured below.

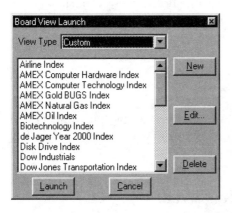

Much like Portfolios, Board Views function in a manner almost completely identical to the Blotter. Just like Blotters, there are Positions Board Views, Quick Board Views, and Custom Board Views. To open an existing Board View (TradeCast includes over 20 with version 3.0) simply highlight one of the Board Views listed under the Custom View Type and click the Launch button. The Board View will appear and you can resize it or edit other attributes just as you would with your Blotter.

Board View [Disk Drive Index]										☒
Symbol	Bid	Ask	Close	Open	Last	Size	Time	Change	High	Low	Volume
APM	7 1/16	7 1/8	7 1/2	7 3/8	7 1/16	200	11:20	-0 7/16	7 3/8	7 1/16	89,500
HMTT	12 9/16	12 5/8	12 1/2	12 1/2	12 5/8	200	11:19	0 1/8	12 7/8	12 1/2	15,900
HTCH	32 5/8	33	32	31 3/4	33	1,300	11:18	1	33 1/4	31 3/4	177,600
IOM	8	8 1/16	7 13/16	7 15/16	8	500	11:20	0 3/16	8 1/8	7 7/8	1,337,100
KMAG	10 13/16	10 15/16	10 15/16	11	10 7/8	500	11:20	-0 1/16	11 1/4	10 7/8	223,900
QNTM	20 7/8	20 15/16	21 5/8	21 7/8	20 7/8	1,000	11:20	-0 3/4	22	20 7/8	800,900
RDRT	16 9/16	16 5/8	16 15/16	16 7/8	16 9/16	100	11:20	-0 3/8	16 7/8	16 1/2	196,600
SEG	31 13/16	31 15/16	32 3/8	32 11/16	31 15/16	1,000	11:20	-0 7/16	32 11/16	31 7/8	523,300
STK	33 1/8	33 3/16	33	33 7/8	33 1/8	2,300	11:20	0 1/8	34	32 3/4	218,000
WDC	15 1/2	15 9/16	15 3/4	15 7/8	15 9/16	500	11:20	-0 3/16	16	15 7/16	313,100

Creating a New Board View

Creating a new Board View is not very dissimilar from creating a new ticker. First open up the Board View Launch window by selecting Board View from the Tools pull-down menu. Click the new button at the right side of the window. You will be prompted to type a name for your new Board View; enter a name and click the OK button with your mouse or press Enter on your keyboard. The Board View Setup window will now appear. This window is identical to the Ticker Setup window—you may add or remove symbols in an identical manner. When you are editing your list of symbols, click the Close button. You will be returned to the Board View Launch window where you can highlight the name of the Board View you wish to open and then click the Launch button, launching the custom Board View as you would any other.

Top Ten

Top 10 windows allow you to easily view the big winners and losers during any given trading day by the market upon which they are traded. Version 3.0 contains the following Top 10 lists depending on the data feed your quote server is on:

PC Quote Feed

Type	Functional
AMEX Gainers/Losers	yes
AMEX Percentage Gainers/Percentage Losers	yes
AMEX Volume	yes
NASDAQ NMS Gainers/Losers	yes
NASDAQ NMS Percentage Gainers/Percentage Losers	yes
NASDAQ NMS Volume	yes

NASDAQ Small Cap Gainers/Losers	yes
NASDAQ Small Cap Percentage Gainers/	
Percentage Losers	yes
NASDAQ Small Cap Volume	yes
NYSE Gainers/Losers	yes
NYSE Percentage Gainers/Percentage Losers	yes
NYSE Volume	yes

S & P Comstock Feed

Type	*Functional*
AMEX Gainers/Losers	yes
AMEX Percentage Gainers/Percentage Losers	(not available)
AMEX Volume	yes
NASDAQ NMS Gainers/Losers	yes
NASDAQ NMS Percentage Gainers/Percentage	
Losers	(not available)
NASDAQ NMS Volume	yes
NASDAQ Small Cap Gainers/Losers	(not available)
NASDAQ Small Cap Percentage Gainers/	
Percentage Losers	(not available)
NASDAQ Small Cap Volume	(not available)
NYSE Gainers/Losers	yes
NYSE Percentage Gainers/Percentage Losers	(not available)
NYSE Volume	yes

Top Ten launch

To launch a Top 10 window, select Top 10 from the Tools pull-down menu, opening the Top 10 Launch window. The window will contain all of the available Top 10 views. Highlight the view you desire to monitor and click the Launch button.

You can resize the window as well as customize its attributes in the same way you customize your Blotter, Board View, or Portfolio.

Fundamental Data Window

The Fundamental Data window displays information about stocks and other securities that is not displayed in Time of Sales, the Blotter, the Stock Window, or any other of version 3.0's many windows. The Fundamental Data window is perhaps the only version 3.0 window that may not be resized or customized due to the specific information that it provides as well as the format of that information.

To open the Fundamental Data window select Fundamental Data from the Tools pull-down menu. The Fundamental Data window will immediately appear. Move the window to the position on your desktop where you would like it to appear.

Type stocks into the Symbol field at the top left side of the window and press the Enter button on your keyboard. The full name of the company will appear to the right of the symbol field; at the same time the Fundamental Data window's four tabs (General, Price/Dividends, Financials, and Earnings) will all be populated with data.

To move amongst the four tabs, simply click once on the label of any particular tab. The information displayed on the tab will be moved to the visible forefront.

Information Displayed in the Fundamental Data Window

The following information is available to you on the four different tabs of the Fundamental Data window:

General Tab	*Price/Dividends Tab*
Cusip	Price Earnings Ratio
SP500	52 Week High/Low
Rank	Year High/Low
SP Stars	Average Daily Volume
Percent Held	Dividend Yield
Beta	Dividend Rate
Option Symbol	Dividend
	Pay Date

Financials Tab	*Earnings*
Balance Sheet Date	Reference Year
Current Assets/Liabilities	Latest Interim Earnings Per Share
Long Term Debt	Current Year Earnings Per Share
Financial Comment	Earnings Comment
Common Shares	Interim Earnings Period
Preferred Shares	last 12-month Earnings Per Share
Leaps	Next Year Est. Earnings

Order Entry Window

The Order Entry is one of the most crucial components of version 3.0. The Order Entry window lets you see the status of all pending orders, whether they are buys, sells, short sells, or cancels in its Pending Orders box. The Order Entry window also displays (in reverse chronological order) a list of executions as well as NASDAQ and Trader messaging in its Activity Log. Open the Order Entry window by selecting Order Entry Window from the Tools pull-down menu or by pressing the spacebar when the Windows focus is on any Stock window. The Order Entry window displays information on orders executed on your workstation. You will receive messages from the Executor as to the status of your order in this window.

The Order Entry window can be resized, but you should be careful when doing so to avoid covering either the Pending Orders box or the Activity Log. If for whatever reason you find all the past messaging that is displayed in the Activity Log turning into "clutter" and making it difficult for you to pick out recently executed trades, you may clear all the trades currently displayed from your Activity Log. Simply right-click on any section of the Order Entry window and select Clear Activity Log.

Customizing the Order Entry Window (Defaults)

The Activity Log section of the Order Entry window can be customized so that certain types of executions and messages are color-coded. This can be done by order/message type (buy, sell, short sell, cancel, and reject) or by market of execution. To set default colors for the five different order/message types, right click anywhere on the Order Entry window (including the Pending Order Box), select Default Color, and then select an order or message. This will open up the Windows color choice options window. Double-click the color you wish the order or message type to appear as. When you are finished selecting a color, click the OK button. Following the above procedure you can assign a different color to all five order/message types so that they will easily be recognizable by color alone in your Activity Log.

Customizing the Order Entry Window (Specific Markets)

When you right click on the Order Entry window, you will notice that above the Default Color selection are Select Net Color, SOES Color, and ISLAND Color selections. You are also able to assign colors so that a SOES buy, a Select Net buy, and an ISLAND buy are all displayed in separate colors in your Activity log. To do so, simply follow the procedure previously described for default Order Entry colors for SOES colors, Select Net colors, and ISLAND colors.

Canceling a Pending order

There are six different ways to cancel a pending order: (Remember, all Select Net orders must be allowed to stay within the system for a minimum of ten seconds. Any attempt to cancel an order before the ten seconds expires will result in a Cancel Rejected message. This NASDAQ rule change affects the Bail Out to SOES feature as well.)

1. At the highlighted Stock Window, hit the Esc key on your keyboard.
2. Press the 'Cancel' button in the bottom center section of a Stock Window.
3. Double click (with the left mouse button) on the pending order only.
4. Press the spacebar on the keyboard to move your focus to the 'pending orders section' on the Order Entry Window. The top pending order will be highlighted in black. Press the escape

key to cancel the order. If there is more than one order, use the up or down arrows on the keyboard to move the highlight to the order you wish to cancel and press cancel.

5. Shift + Esc key. (Focus[1] on Stock Window) cancels all pending orders for that security.
6. Shift + Esc key. (Focus[1] on Order Entry window) cancels <u>all</u> pending orders.

Manually Entered Trades

Trades that are manually entered by the Broker Dealer into your Account will show up as reversed out.

```
┌─────────────────────────────────────────────────┐
│ Order Entry                                  [x] │
│ ┌─ Pending Orders ──────────────────────────────┐│
│ │┌─────────────────────────────────────────────┐││
│ ││                                             │││
│ ││                                             │││
│ ││                                             │││
│ ││                                             │││
│ ││                                             │││
│ │└─────────────────────────────────────────────┘││
│ ┌─ Activity Log ────────────────────────────────┐│
│ │MOE Removed Sold EBAY 200 at 100               ││
│ │MOE Added Bought EBAY 500 at 171               ││
│ │Short Sold SelectNet EBAY 200 100 MWSE 16:10:40││
│ │Short Sold SelectNet EBAY 500 172 TNTO 16:10:39││
│ │Sold SOES MSFT 1000 132 1/8  13:53:39          ││
│ │Sold SOES DELL 1000 67 11/16  13:53:38         ││
│ │TCAST REJ - EXCEEDS SOES TIER LIMIT 200 Sell SOE││
│ │TCAST REJ - EXCEEDS SOES TIER LIMIT 200 Sell SOE││
│ │Bought Island TGLO 1000 36 1/2  13:52:53       ││
│ │Bought Island EWBX 1000 48 3/4  13:49:55       ││
│ │Bought Island DELL 1000 67 5/8  13:07:36       ││
│ │Bought Island MSFT 1000 131 5/8  13:07:23      ││
│ └───────────────────────────────────────────────┘│
└─────────────────────────────────────────────────┘
```

Alert Windows

Version 3.0 includes several alerts to make you aware of trading opportunities that occur during any given trading day in securities that you may not be aware of or do not regularly trade. The High/Low alert counts the new highs and lows for ALL NASDAQ and NYSE stocks while the Inside Quote alert counts consecutive up-ticks and down-ticks on the bid side of a stock's inside quote. Either alert may be opened by selecting Alerts from the Tools pull-down menu and then selecting either High/Low or Inside Quote. Both windows may be resized as needed to fit your layout.

[1] When you click on a given window in version 3.0 the window becomes boldly outlined. When a window appears as such, it is said to have the **focus.**

High/Low & Inside Quote Alert Window Setup

As described previously, the High/Low alert window scans all NAS-DAQ and NYSE stocks for new highs and lows and numbers them consecutively so that you can tell which stocks keep breaking through to new levels and which keep getting stopped dead in their tracks. There are, however, a great number of NYSE and NASDAQ stocks so you will likely want to set some filters so you're only updated to new highs and lows in securities that fit your trading style.

High/Low Alert

To open the High/Low Alert Setup window either double-click the High/Low alert window or right-click the window and choose Setup.

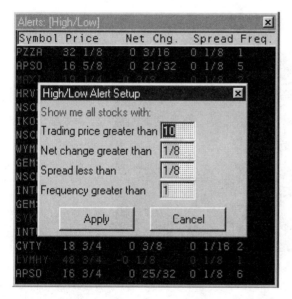

Enter the lowest price for a stock that you would trade in the Trading Price Greater Than field. This will make sure that you're not bombarded with alerts about stocks whose trading price is too low to warrant much interest. To avoid seeing alerts telling you that a stock that is up a ¹⁄₁₆ for the day has hit a new high, enter a value appropriate to your style of trading in the Net Change Greater Than field. For example, entering ½ for the value in that field means you would only be alerted to new highs and lows in stocks that are up or down at least a ½ point for the day. Many traders like to only trade stocks with a tight spread while others view a ½ spread no differently than a

$\frac{1}{16}$ spread. Enter the largest spread you would still trade in the Spread Less Than field. Almost every stock will have several highs and lows for any given trading day. Enter the number of highs or lows that need to occur **BEFORE** the High/Low Alert window begins to update every time a new high or low is reached in the Frequency Greater Than field. Please note that depending on what values you initially enter, you will very likely want update the values as the trading day progresses.

Inside Quote Alert

To open the Inside Quote Alert Setup window either double-click the High/Low alert window or right-click the window and choose Setup.

Alerts: [Inside Quote]					☒
Symbol	**Bid**	**Ask**	**Net**	**Chg.**	**#Bid**
AAPL	26 7/16	26 1/2	6	11/16	-1
CYRK	10 3/4	10 7/8	-0	1/4	0
AAPL	26 3/8	26 1/2	6	13/16	-2
ALTR	64 9/16	64 11/16	0	11/16	1
AORI	15 9/16	15 3/4	-0	1/8	1
CHRT	15 1/2	15 3/4	0	1/8	0
CBRL	28 1/2	28 5/8	0	1/8	1
QCOM	47 7/8	48	0	1/8	-1
WAMU	68 1/2	68 3/4	1	1/8	-1
ADBE	40 3/4	41	1	11/16	-1
CELL	30 15/16	31 1/8	-0	3/16	0
PRDE	27	27 1/4	1		1
SDTI	42 1/2	42 3/4	3	1/4	1
BHARr	70 1/2	70 1/8	3	3/4	-2
TLAB	62	62 1/8	1	1/4	1
AMAT	94 13/16	94 7/8	-1	1/8	1
JBIL	52 1/2	52 3/4	0	15/16	-2

Just like the High/Low Alert window, you will want to apply some filters to your Inside Quote Alert window to avoid being unnecessarily updated about a stock that does not fit your style of trading.

The Bid Price Greater Than/Less than fields allow you to set a range for the price of stocks that you are willing to trade. Enter the smallest price for a stock you would consider trading in the first field and the highest price for a stock you would be willing to trade in the second field. Enter a value for the minimum amount that the price of the stock must have changed since opening that day in the Net Change Greater Than field. To avoid entering a position on a stock that is not trading but whose price is being frequently updated, enter a value for the minimum number if shares that must have traded in a stock before you are alerted to inside quote changes. The main purpose of the Inside Quote window is to count consecutive up-ticks or down-ticks on the bid side of the inside quote. Enter the least number of consecutive up or down ticks that must occur before you are alerted in the # of Consecutive Ticks On Bid field.

Setting Alert Window Fonts

The font used for both the High/Low Alert and Inside Quote Alert window is customizable. To launch the font setup window for both alerts, right-click on the window and chooses font. This will open the standard Windows font setup window. Here you may change the font and font size for that alert window's display. The High/Low alert has an additional customizable display setting. By right clicking on the High/Low alert window and selecting colors. Added filters to Inside Quote Ticker: Now you are able to scan all 6500+ NASDAQ securities for inside quote changes *while* filtering the information by price, net change in price for the day, volume for the day, and consecutive up-ticks/down-ticks.

Added a customizable High/Low Alerts: Track new highs and lows for all NASDAQ stocks. The ticker allows traders to custom filter stocks by their price, change in price for the day, and spread. Most importantly, it counts highs and lows so traders can separate false alarms from real trade opportunities and spot market divergences with ease.

Remember: The Inside Quote and High /Low Alerts are designed to work within an office without any problems. However, the Insider will not work over the Internet or RAS. In Wide Area Network applications; ISDN, Direct 56 circuits, etc., port settings must be turned on to allow data to flow across. Contact you network administrator for further details.

Baskets

Opening the Baskets Window

The Basket window is home to some of the most powerful functionality that version 3.0 has to offer. The Baskets window will let you close **ALL** of your open positions or establish multiple new positions in preset groups that you assemble.

Selecting Baskets from the Tools pull-down menu will open the Baskets window. Order Entry via the Baskets window will be discussed fully later in this help guide.

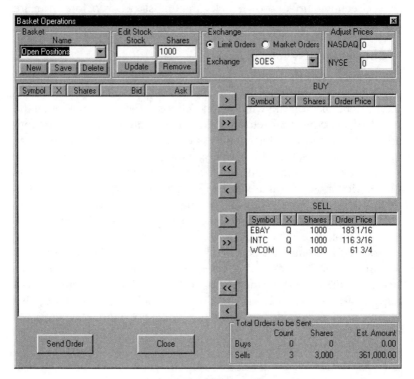

Basket
- Name
  - Open Positions (Default)
  - Long Positions
  - Short Positions
- Any customized baskets
- New—Lets you set up a new basket of stocks
- Save—saves your current baskets
- Delete—deletes the current basket

Edit
- Stock—the stock symbols you wish to add, modify or remove

- Shares—the number for the order for that stock
- Update—adds the current stock and shares to the buy or sell section, or adds it to the unassigned symbol list.
- Remove—Deletes the current stock and shares to the buy or sell section, or deletes it from the unassigned symbol list.

Exchange
- Limit Orders—will send out all stocks in the buy or sell section as a limit order, whenever the user clicks on send.
- Market Orders—will send out all stocks in the buy or sell section as a market order, whenever the user clicks on send.
- Exchange selection box—selects the market on which NASDAQ orders are sent out (SOES, SelectNet, ISLAND.

Adjust Prices
- NASDAQ the price amount that will be added or subtracted from an OTC limit order (buy/sell).
- NYSE the price amount that will be added or subtracted from an Listed limit order (buy/sell).

Unassigned symbol list
- The large section of the basket window that contains stocks that have yet to be assigned to a buy or sell section.
- Symbol—stock symbol
- X—exchange code
- Shares—number of shares
- Bid—bid when the basket was pulled up
- Ask—ask when the basket was pulled up

Buy
- Symbol—stock symbol
- X—exchange code
- Shares—number of shares
- Order Price—the price at which the order will be sent or MKT if market is selected

Sell
- Symbol—stock symbol
- X—exchange code
- Shares—number of shares

- Order Price—the price at which the order will be sent or MKT if market is selected

Total orders to be sent
- A summary of all the buys, sells, shares, and estimated amount that will be sent if the send order button is pressed.

Send Order Button
- The button that will allow you to send all orders loaded in either the buy or sell section. A progress bar will pop up displaying the status of the pending orders

Close Button
- This button allows you to close the Basket window without sending any orders.

5. General Customization

Under the File menu, Setup, General, is the Trader Setup window. The first field on the Trader Setup window is User Files Path. This is a listing of the path on your computer or local network where version 3.0 will look for information concerning layouts, keystrokes, and order entry defaults. If you are an Internet trader or you trade in an office that doesn't store all user files on a local file server you will likely never need to change these settings.

Trader Setup	☒
User Files Path: ST\TRADER\User Files	Browse...
Speed keys File:	▼
Link App Caption:	☐ Link Graphs
Display	
☑ News Messages from Executor	Save
☑ Trades on Insider	Cancel

Speed Keys

The Speed Keys File field contains the ticker file you will use as a speed keys file. All available ticker files are listed here and can be accessed by left-clicking on the downward pointing triangle, highlighting the desired ticker file, and releasing the left mouse button.

Link App Caption

If you wish to link all your Stock Windows to an external charting program such as RealTick III you will need to specify that link here and click the "Link Graphs" checkbox.

The Display area contains two checkboxes. If you would like your Trader workstation to alert you of any status messages from the Executor i.e. "Lost Connection to SOES Server", "You Have Been Switched to trader Mode" check the box next to "News Messages from the Executor". Otherwise, leave the button unchecked—but be wary. You may later be counting on the availability of a particular market for an execution only to find the server temporarily unavailable and yourself unaware because you disabled the messaging.

Order Entry Setup

The Order Entry Setup window is made up of two sections, Order Entry and Exchange Default.

The Order Entry Tab

The Order Entry Tab is made up of three separate areas—General, NASDAQ Settings, and Required Confirmations.

```
Order Entry Setup                                    ☒

 | Order Entry | Exchange Defaults |

  ┌─ General ──────────────────────────────────┐
  │   ☑ Use Order Entry KeyStrokes             │
  │   Default Shares:  [1000    ]              │
  └────────────────────────────────────────────┘
  ┌─ NASDAQ Settings ──────────────────────────┐
  │   Default Market on NASDAQ:  [SOES    ▼]   │
  │   ☐ Preference ECN Based Upon Size         │
  └────────────────────────────────────────────┘
  ┌─ Required Confirmations ───────────────────┐
  │   ☐ Before exceeding default shares amount.│
  │   ☑ Before sending short sell +1/16        │
  │   ☐ Require Confirmation Before Sending Orders│
  └────────────────────────────────────────────┘

        [  Save  ]      [  Cancel  ]
```

General

Use Order Entry Keystrokes

If you wish to input orders into version 3.0 using the keyboard, check the "Use Order Entry Keystrokes" box. If you wish to use the mouse simply leave the box unchecked. Enter your preferred number of default shares into the Default Share Box.

Version 3.0 will send out every order for this number of shares unless a different number is specified. As the SOES market has a 1000 share maximum we would highly suggest leaving this value at or less then 1000 if you plan on executing any orders whatsoever on SOES.

Default Shares

Allows you to specify the number of default shares loaded in all Stock Windows.

NASDAQ Settings

Default NASDAQ Market

Use the pull-down menu labeled "Default Market on NASDAQ" to specify either SOES or Select Net as the market to send NASDAQ orders to unless otherwise specified.

Preference ECN Based upon Size

Often when sending orders, there is more then one ECN at the Inside Bid or Ask where are you trying to execute a Direct ECN buy or Sell. If the "Preference ECN Based Upon Size" box is checked, all Direct ECN Buys or Sells will be sent to whichever ECN at the Inside Bid or Ask has more available shares.

Required Confirmations

The three checkboxes under Required Confirmations are situations when, if the box is checked, you will be presented with a Yes or No dialogue box you will be forced to respond to before sending an order. While more experienced traders may find this somewhat annoying or intrusive, TradeCast recommends newer traders check these boxes until they become intimately familiar with the results and ramifications of the many different order types Trader Pro is capable of.

Before exceeding default shares amount

Check here to receive warning before exceeding the specified default share amount.

Before sending short sell +¹⁄₁₆

A message box will pop up asking whether you are sure you would like to send the order out a ¹⁄₁₆ above the Best Bid. This will happen only if the option is checked, otherwise the order will automatically be adjusted ¹⁄₁₆ above and sent.

Required Confirmations

A Yes or No dialogue box you will be forced to respond to before sending an order. As with changes made to many of the other version 3.0 customization and setup menus, you will need to be sure and left-click the Save button to apply changes that you have made. Left-clicking cancel or closing the setup box in any other manner without first clicking Save will cancel all changes made.

Exchange Defaults Tab

The Exchange Defaults tab lets you set SOES defaults, Select Net defaults NYSE Defaults, and ISLAND defaults.

Exchanges

The Exchange section allows you to set up customized options for each market available to you. This includes SOES, SelectNet, and ISLAND on the NASDAQ exchange. New York Stock Exchange and American Stock Exchange executions available on the NYSE exchange.

```
Order Entry Setup                                    [×]

  Order Entry   Exchange Defaults

            Exchange     [SOES          ▼]
                         ┌─────────────────┐
                         │ SOES            │
  Order Type    [Limit   │ SelectNet       │
                         │ Island          │
  All Or None   [Partial │ NYSE            │ es [0  ]
                         └─────────────────┘
  Time In Force [Day          ▼]  Minutes    [0  ]




              [  Save  ]    [  Cancel  ]
```

SOES

Operation Hours (9:30 am – 4:00 pm ET)

Overview of SOES

(Small Order Execution System) SOES is an automated trading system that lets SOES participants enter and execute orders of limited size in active SOES-authorized NASDAQ securities. Reports of these executions are sent to the Automated Confirmation Transaction (ACT) Service as locked-in trades, then both sides of the transaction are sent to the applicable clearing corporation(s) for clearance and settlement, and the trade is reported to the tape.

Both NASDAQ National Market and the NASDAQ SmallCap Market securities are eligible for trading through SOES. The stocks are separated into tiers representing the largest order for a given stock that can be entered into SOES. National Market securities are separated into tiers of 200, 500, and 1000. Shares, depending on the trading characteristics of the stock. SmallCap securities are separated into 100- or 500-share tiers.

All order-entry firms and Market Makers registered with NASDAQ have access to SOES, but Electronic Communications Network (ECN) and unlisted trading privileges (UTP) participant quotes are not accessible through SOES.

The National Association of Securities Dealers and Quotations created this system to allow investors fair access to the market. This system was enacted after the crash of 1987.

Hours of Operation

SOES orders priced as "market" may be entered into the system beginning at system open (7:30 am ET) for execution at market open (9:30 am ET). Marketable limit orders and market orders may be entered into SOES during the normal market hours of 9:30 am to 4:00 pm, ET.

Types of Orders allowed

Market
Limit
All or none (AON)
Fill or kill (FOK)
Good till Canceled (GTC)

SOES operation in locked/crossed markets

During normal conditions, a market maker has 17 seconds between SOES executions. When the market in a security is locked or crossed, SOES will continue to execute orders; however, in a locked/crossed market, there will be only a five-second period between SOES executions.

SelectNet

Operation Hours (9:00 am – 9:30 am; 9:30 am – 4:00 pm; and 4:00 pm – 5:15 pm ET)

Overview of SelectNet

SelectNet offers traders the ability to automate the negotiation and execution of trades. Orders of any size up to six digits can be traded on SelectNet. Executions are automatically reported to ACT for public dissemination and sent to clearing for comparison and settlement.

SelectNet allows order entry firms and Market Makers to direct orders to specified Market Makers, UTP participants, or ECN's, or to broadcast orders to all participants quoting the issue. SelectNet also identifies incoming and outgoing orders and allows you to see subsequent messaging and negotiation results.

SelectNet has been designated as the vehicle to link the NASDAQ market with ECN's for application of the SEC Order Handling Rules. Participants may preference orders in SelectNet to a particular ECN for execution, but no special condition orders are allowed into SelectNet for routing to an ECN. Special conditions include: all or none, non-negotiable orders, and orders that include a minimum acceptance quantity for execution.

You may not cancel or attempt to cancel a SelectNet order for 10 seconds after you enter the order. This rule applies to orders entered during all three sessions of the SelectNet operation hours.

SelectNet operations within a Locked and Crossed market

When the best bid equals the best offer or when the best bid is higher than the best offer, the market maker is considered to be 'locked' or 'crossed.' Market Makers and ECN's are required by NAS-DAQ to enter and maintain quotations in NASDAQ that

ISLAND

The Island is an Electronic Communications Network (ECN).

Operation Hours (9:00 am – 9:30 am; 9:30 am – 4:00 pm; and 4:00 pm – 5:15 pm ET)

NYSE

The New York Stock Exchange

Operation Hours (9:00 am – 9:30 am; 9:30 am – 4:00 pm)

AMEX

The American Stock Exchange

Operation Hours (9:00 am – 9:30 am; 9:30 am – 4:00 pm)

CBOT

The Chicago Board of Trade

CME

The Chicago Mercantile Exchange

Electronic Communications Networks (ECNs)

INCA, ISLD, TNTO, BTRD, BRUT, REDI, & ATTN

Exchange Default Terminology

Time in Force (TIF)	The length of time in minutes an order remains live.
Fill or Kill Order (FOK)	must immediately be filled in its entirety, or, if this is not possible, the order is cancelled. This designation requires All or None to be set to All or None.
Market (Mkt)	Order is sent to execute as soon as possible at the prevailing market price.
Limit	for a limit order, a single price is entered. The execution price cannot exceed the limit price on a buy, or be lower on a sell.
Stop	for a stop order, a single price is entered. Once the stock price reaches or passes that level a market order is entered.
Stop Limit	requires a stop price and a limit price. Similar to a stop order, except that when the stop price is reached, a limit order is placed at the limit price.
Partial	execute the order for any number of shares up to the total shares ordered.
All or None (AON)	selecting this option means that whenever you send an order you are unwilling to accept a partial fill, and will only allow a market maker or ECN to fill your order in its entirety.
Use Minimum	accept partial fills as long as they exceed a specified minimum

	number of shares. This type of All or None requires the minimum number of shares to be set.
Day	order is only valid for the current day; thus it expires if not executed on the day it is placed.
At Close	the order is to be executed at the market close by a specialist, or cancelled if unable to execute.
Use Specific Minutes	the order is valid for a specific number of minutes. This type of time in force requires the time in force minutes to be set.
Market on Close	A market order to be executed just prior to the close of a trading session, or cancelled if execution is not possible.
Immediate or Cancel (IOC)	Order is placed for immediate execution and then withdrawn whether or not it has been completely filled. This designation requires All or None to be set to Partial.

Linking Windows

One of the most important improvements to version 3.0 is its ability to link various version 3.0 windows together. Now when a new stock appears in a Top 10 Gainer board view you can pull it up on a TradeChart, Stock Window, and Time of Sales Window in one simple click of the mouse. Linking multiple version 3.0 windows is discussed in this help guide.

TradeCast has dramatically changed the way in which Time and Sales windows links to Stock Windows in order to accommodate the linking of Stock Windows to the new TradeCharts application. First, open your previously saved layout or create a new one. Type a symbol into the Market maker boxes, but DO NOT type any symbols into the TOS windows. After all windows are open, select Linking from the File, Setup, Links pull-down menu.

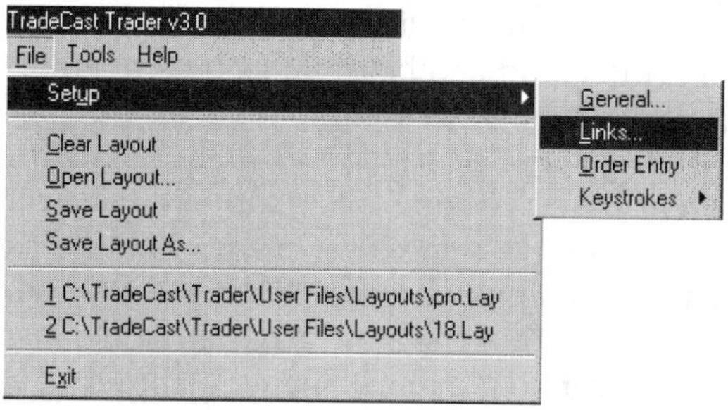

TradeCast Trader v3.0
File   Tools   Help

Setup	▶	General...
Clear Layout		Links...
Open Layout...		Order Entry
Save Layout		Keystrokes ▶
Save Layout As...		

1 C:\TradeCast\Trader\User Files\Layouts\pro.Lay
2 C:\TradeCast\Trader\User Files\Layouts\18.Lay

Exit

All of your TOS and Stock Windows will be listed as illustrated below, in the order they were opened.

Link Window ☒

TradeCast Link Groups: 1 ▼

1--DELL
1--TOS

Set Link   Cancel

Links between TOS windows and Stock Windows are now sorted into GROUPS. Any time you enter a symbol into a Stock Window, any TOS AS WELL AS any Stock Windows in the same group (assuming more than one Stock Window has been assigned to the group) will automatically jump to that symbol.

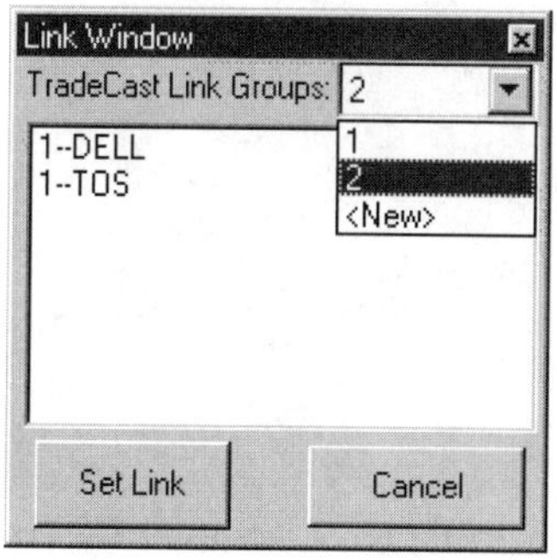

Link Window ☒

TradeCast Link Groups: 2 ▼

1--DELL   1
1--TOS   2
               <New>

Set Link   Cancel

To assign windows to a group, simply click the window title with the mouse. This will change the group number from its present group to the next logical group, assigning it to that group. Initially, no windows have been assigned groups and all windows will be labeled as belonging to group 0. From there, clicking on a window title will switch it to group 1. When you have selected as many windows as you would like to belong to a given group, simply select <New> from the TradeCast Link groups field. You will now have an additional group number that you may assign to the remaining non-labeled windows. You may create a theoretically unlimited number of groups, but around 15-20 groups you may start running into CPU and/or RAM limitations, depending on the quality of your workstation.

When you are done assigning groups, simply click the Set Link button.

6. Order Entry Using a Mouse

NASDAQ ORDER ENTRY

Order Entry with a Mouse

There are two ways in which you can execute SOES trades. The Function Keys or the mouse execution system using the load section illustrated below. New Order Entry Section lets you know what order you are about to send without all the guessing. To access the Mouse settings for order entry, simply press on the gray up arrow located in the lower left corner of the stock window. When an Item is grayed out, it does not affect the order. For Example SOES orders do not use Stop Price, Order Time, All or None, Minutes, or Preference as the following picture demonstrates.

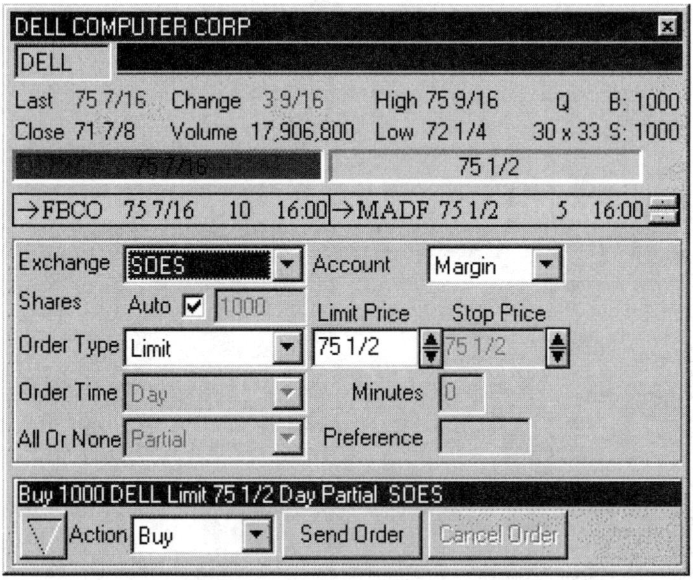

SOES Order Entry (Available Fields)

Exchange
- SOES

Shares
- Auto
- User select

Order Type (SOES Only)
- Limit
- Market

Limit Price
- Scroll or type in the price

Order Time (SelectNet or ISLAND)
- Day
- At Close

- Use Specific Minutes
- Immediate or Cancel (Island Only)

Account
- Cash
- Margin
- Short

Fields Not Available
- Order time
- All or None
- Minutes
- Preference
- Stop Price

SelectNet Order Entry (Available Fields)

Exchange
- SelectNet

Shares
- Auto
- User select

Order Time
- Day
- At Close

- Use Specific Minutes
    - Minutes

All or None
- Partial
- All or None
- Use Minimum

Account
- Cash
- Margin
- Short

Preference
- Market Makers MMID for preferencing.

Fields Not Available
- Order Type
- Stop Price

Island Order Entry (Available Fields)

Exchange
- Island ECN

Shares
- Auto
- User select

Order Time
  • Day
  • A Close
  • Use Specific Minutes
    • minutes
  • Immediate or Cancel
Account
  • Margin
  • Short
  • Cash
Fields Not Available
  • Order Type
  • All or None
  • Stop Price
  • Preference

NYSE Order Entry

NYSE Order Entry with a Mouse

There are two ways in which you can execute NYSE trades. The
Function Keys or the mouse execution system using the load section

INTL BUSINESS MACHINES CORP   [x]

IBM

Last 185   Change 2 3/4   High185 3/8   N   B: 1000
Close 182 1/4   Volume 3,535,000 Low 181 1/8   5 x 15 S: 1000

T MMID Price   Sz   Time T MMID Price   Sz   Time
↑ NYSE 185 1/16   10   16:00 ↓ PACF   185   15   16:35
↑ NASD 184 15/16   1   16:15 ↑ NYSE   185 3/16   10   16:00
↑ PHLX 184 15/16   1   16:18

Exchange NYSE   Account   Margin
Shares   Auto ✓ 1000   Limit Price   Stop Price
Order Type Limit
Order Time Day   Minutes 3
All Or None Partial   Preference

Buy 1000 IBM Limit Day Partial NYSE
      Action Buy   Send Order   Cancel Order

illustrated below. **New Order Entry Section** lets you know what order you are about to send without all the guessing.

New York Order Entry (Available Fields)

Exchange
- (Default NYSE when NYSE or AMEX stock is entered in stock window)

Shares
- Auto
- User select

Order Type
- Market
- Limit
- Stop
- Stop Limit
- Market on Close

Order Time
- Day
- Fill or Kill
- Immediate or Cancel

All or None
- Partial
- All or None

Account
- Cash
- Margin
- Short

Fields Not Available
- Minutes
- Preference

7. Order Entry using Keystroke

By Default, TradeCast is programmed with Order Entry Keystrokes. Keystroke Order Entry is not designed for the novice trader. It is a very powerful way to place and execute orders on the various exchanges. To turn on keystroke order entry, simply access the File, Setup section in the Trader Bar. In the Order Entry Tab, select Use Order Entry Keystrokes by placing a check in the box with a click of the mouse.

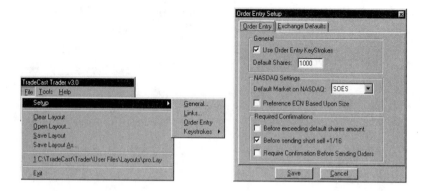

Order Entry

These functions will only happen when either the Order Entry Window or the Stock Window is Highlighted (Windows focus is on it).

Space   Switch back to Stock Window
Esc   Cancel Selected Order
Shift-Esc   Cancel All pending orders

Keystroke Customization

To change the F1 through F12 Order Entry Keys, simply access the Trader 3.0 Bar and go to File, Setup, Keystrokes, OTC (NASDAQ-SOES, Select Net, ISLAND) or Listed (NYSE and AMEX).

Listed Keystrokes

To change the F1 through F12 Order Entry Keys, double-click on the keystroke you wish to change. Follow the Prompt to create a new Keystroke.

These keystrokes will either bring up a load section to send an order, or directly send the order to the exchange. These are Defaults and may be changed by the end user.

Key	Action	Description
F1	Sends	a **Mkt Sell** to NYSE/AMEX at the market price.
F2	Sends	a **Market on Close Sell** to NYSE/AMEX at the market price.
F3	Sends	a **Limit Sell** to NYSE/AMEX at the best bid minus price adjustment (default = ¼).
F4	Sends	a **Limit Sell** to NYSE/AMEX at the best bid.
F5	Sends	a **Market Short Sell** to NYSE/AMEX at the market price.
F6	Loads	a **Limit Short Sell** to NYSE/AMEX at the best bid, then the user selects price, shares, adjustments, enter to send.
F7	Loads	a **Limit Sell** to NYSE/AMEX at the best bid, then the user selects price, shares, adjustments, enter to send.
F8	Loads	a **Limit Buy** to NYSE/AMEX at the best ask, then the user selects price, shares, adjustments, enter to send.
F9	Sends	a **Limit Buy** to NYSE/AMEX at the best ask.
F10	Sends	a **Limit Buy** to NYSE/AMEX at the best ask plus price adjustment (default = ¼).
F12	Sends	a Market buy to NYSE/AMEX at the market price.

Preview Keystrokes

To preview OTC the Keystroke you have just created, simply click on the Preview Tab.

Print Keystrokes

To print this template to a Network Printer, right mouse-click in the white area above and select print. This will allow you to create a custom template that you can tape on the keyboard just above the F1-F12 Keystrokes.

OTC Keystrokes

To change the F1 through F12 Order Entry Keys, double-click on the keystroke you wish to change. Follow the Prompt to create a new Keystroke.

OTC Keystroke Detail

These keystrokes will either bring up a load section to send an order, or directly send the order to the exchange. These are Defaults and may be changed by the end user.

Key	Action	Description
F1	Sends	a **MKT SELL** to the SOES system at the Market Price.
F2	Sends	a FOK **Sell** on the ISLAND ECN at Best BID on Level I BID.
F3	Sends	a **LIMIT SELL** at the Best BID on Level I minus Price adjustment (default = $\frac{1}{8}$).

F4	Sends	a **LIMIT SELL** at the Best BID.
F5	Sends	a **Short SELL** at the **MKT** to the SOES system at the BID.
F6	Loads	a **Short OFFER** at the best ask on Level I to IS-LAND ECN.
F7	Loads	an **OFFER** at the best ask on Level I to ISLAND ECN.
F8	Loads	a **BID** at the best bid on Level I to the ISLAND ECN.
F9	Sends	a **BUY** order at the best ask on level I to the SOES system.
F10	Sends	a **BUY** order at the best ask on level I plus price adjustment (default = $\frac{1}{8}$).
F11	Sends	a FOK **BID** at the best ask on Level I to the ISLAND ECN.
F12	Sends	a **MKT BUY** order to the SOES system Market Price.

Ctrl Keystrokes

Hold Down the Ctrl Key and then press either F1 through F12. These keystrokes will either bring up a load section to send an order, or directly send the order to the exchange. These are Defaults and may be changed by the end user.

Key	*Action*	*Description*
F1	Sends	a preference limit sell at the best bid to an ECN (by size or first in) on SelectNet.
F2	Loads	a preference limit sell to a market maker (default: Set to first MM, then user select) at the mm price.
F3		If you are long or hedged one share, this swipe will load multiple limit sells preferenced to each market maker at their current price, and shares of 1000, or the shares amount you specify. If you are flat, this swipe will load multiple limit short sells preferenced to multiple market makers at their current price, and shares of 1000, or the shares amount you specify.
F5	Sends	a limit short sell at the best bid/level I on the IS-LAND ECN.
F6	Loads	a **Short OFFER** at the best ask/level 1on SelectNet.
F7	Loads	an **OFFER** at the best ask/level 1on SelectNet.

F8   <u>Loads</u>   a **BID** at the best bid/level 1on SelectNet.
F10   this swipe will load multiple limit buys, preferenced to market makers at a selected level at their current price, and shares of 1000, or the shares amount you specify.
F11   <u>Loads</u>   a preference limit buy at the market makers price (default: Set to first MM, then user select).
F12   Sends   a preference limit buy to an ECN (by size or first in) on SelectNet at the best ask.

Ctrl & ALT Combination Keystrokes

(Hold Down the Ctrl Key & the Alt Key then press either F1 through F12)

Key   *Description*

F3   If you are long or hedged one share, this monster swipe <u>loads</u> multiple preferenced limit sells to individual market makers at the bid price and shares the market makers are posting. After the MMID and Price is highlighted (blue), hit the 'enter' key on keyboard to send order. If you are flat, this monster swipe <u>loads</u> multiple preferenced limit short sells to individual market makers at the bid price and shares the market makers are posting. After the MMID and Price are highlighted (blue), hit the 'enter' key on keyboard to send order.
F10   This monster swipe <u>loads</u> multiple preferenced limit buys to individual market makers at the offer price and shares the market makers are posting. After the MMID and Price is highlighted (blue), hit the 'enter' key on keyboard to send order.

Island Buy FOK Plus & Island Sell FOK Minus

When a stock is ripping up and you want to buy it. You can send a Island Buy FOK from the loaded offer price plus an $\frac{1}{16}$, $\frac{1}{8}$, or $\frac{1}{4}$. When a stock is ripping down and you want to sell it. You can send a Island Sell FOK from the loaded Bid price minus an $\frac{1}{16}$, $\frac{1}{8}$, or $\frac{1}{4}$. These two keystrokes are useful when the market is locked or crossed.

TradeCast has created two new orders with no keystrokes attached within the OTC keystrokes setup. These two keystrokes allow you to send out orders plus or minus

Preview Keystrokes

To preview the Keystroke you have just created, simply click on the Preview Tab.

Preview Window										
Key	oes Mkt Se	ld Sell FO	bes Sell Lin	bes Limit S		es Mkt Sh	d Short Off	Isld Offer	Isld Bid		es Limit Bu	bs Limit Bu
Ctrl	N ECN Se	N Load Off	Offer Swi		Isld Short	Short Off	SN Offer	SN Bid		N Bid Swip	N Load Bid
Alt	Load ECN										
Ctrl+Alt			Monster O								Monster E

Print Keystrokes

To print this template to a Network Printer, right mouse-click in the white area above and select print. This will allow you to create a custom template that you can tape on the keyboard just above the F1-F12 Keystrokes.

Other Features of Keystroke Order Entry

SOES Lean

All SOES market orders are leaned by the system. Whenever you have entered a SOES market order only to find the SOESable market maker disappear and be replaced by an ECN, NASDAQ holds the order in a queue until a SOESable market maker becomes available or the order is cancelled.

Select Net Override Price

TradeCast Trader will automatically send the order to Select Net system with a price override flag for prices that are under the bid or above the offer. A warning message is displayed for both Select Net/ISLAND if you try to bid above the ask or offer below the bid. This will also allow you to get your order out when the market is locked or crossed.

Order Entry Setup

Order Entry | Exchange Defaults

Exchange   [SelectNet ▼]

Order Type   [Limit ▼]

All Or None   [All or None ▼]   Min Shares [0]

Time In Force   [Use Specific t ▼]   Minutes [3]

SelectNet
☐ Auto Override Price

[Save]   [Cancel]

Action	Price	Select Net Override	Notes
Bid	< Best Bid	Yes	Automatic override on Select Net
Bid	> Best Ask	No	System will ask you:

A Message pops up: "You are about to bid above the market. Do you want to continue?"

At this point you can press to 'Y' to continue or 'N' to cancel.

			If you want to override or not.
Offer	> Best Ask	Yes	Auto override
Offer	< Best Bid	No	System will ask you:

A message pops up: "You are about to offer below the market. Do you want to continue?"

Swipe

Traders who take advantage of speed keys built into version 3.0 have two exciting new methods of placing orders. Pressing CTRL+ F3 simultaneously is the Offer Swipe. It will send a preferred Select Net offer to all market makers at the price they are posting in 1000 share lots. Conversely, pressing CTRL+ F10 simultaneously is the Bid Swipe. This action will send a preferred Select Net bid to all market makers at the inside offer in 1000 share lots. Please note that once one of your Select Net offers or bids placed via this function is filled, your remaining orders are NOT automatically cancelled. Please refer to the next section for information on new speed keys for canceling orders.

Monster Swipe

Traders who take advantage of speed keys built into version 3.0 have two exciting new methods of placing orders. Pressing CTRL & Alt & F3 simultaneously is the Monster Offer Swipe. It will send a preferred Select Net offer to all market makers at the price and shares amount each Market Maker is posting. Conversely, pressing CTRL & Alt & F10 simultaneously is the Monster Bid Swipe. This action will send a preferred Select Net bid to all market makers at the inside offer bid, at the share amount each Market Maker is posting. Please note that once one of your Select Net offers or bids placed via this function is filled, your remaining orders are NOT automatically cancelled. Please refer to the next section for information on new speed keys for canceling orders.

8. Canceling a Pending order

There are six different ways to cancel a pending order: (Remember, all Select Net orders must be allowed to stay within the system for a minimum of ten seconds. Any attempt to cancel an order before the ten seconds expires will result in a Cancel Rejected message. This NASDAQ rule change affects the Bail Out to SOES feature as well.)

```
Order Entry                                              [x]
┌Pending Orders───────────────────────────────────────────
│Bidding SelectNet...  KLAC 1000  28 1/16  18:57:41 0 14




│

┌Activity Log─────────────────────────────────────────────
│Bought SelectNet HBOC 1000  58 5/16  18:57:17
│Bought SOES BMCS 1000  49 7/8  18:56:57
│Bought SelectNet LIPO 1000  5 13/16 DTEK 18:55:13
│Bought SelectNet LIPO 1000  5 13/16  18:54:58
│Bought SOES STAR 1000  15 3/8  18:54:22
│Short Sold Island ZITL 1000  7 11/32  18:54:12
│Bought Island QCOM 1000  51 1/4  18:53:52
│Bought SOES ORCL 1000  24 7/8  18:53:29
│TCAST REJ - SIX MIN. SHARES LEFT 0 Buy ASND 1000  45  18:53:13 0 5
│Bought Island ASND 1000  44 15/16  18:53:02
│Bought SelectNet FORE 1000  22 5/16  18:52:48
```

1. At the highlighted Stock Window, hit the Esc key on your keyboard.
2. Press the 'Cancel' button in the bottom center section of a Stock Window.
3. Double click (with the left mouse button) on the pending order only.
4. Press the spacebar on the keyboard to move your focus to the 'pending orders section' on the Order Entry Window. The top pending order will be highlighted in black. Press the escape key to cancel the order. If there is more than one order, use the up or down arrows on the keyboard to move the highlight to the order you wish to cancel and press cancel.
5. Shift + Esc key. (Focus[2] on Stock Window) cancels all pending orders for that security.
6. Shift + Esc key. (Focus[2] on Order Entry window) cancels <u>all</u> pending orders.

---

[2] Whenever you click on a given window in version 3.0 the window becomes boldly outlined. When a window appears as such, it is said to have the **focus.**

Glossary

advance/decline line   A measure of market movements of securities prices composed of the cumulative total of differences between advancing issues (stocks whose prices are up on the day) and declining issues (stocks whose prices are down on the day).

ask   The lowest currently stated acceptable price for a specific stock or commodity on the floor of an exchange. Also called the offer.

at-the-money   An option in which the price of the underlying instrument is exactly the same as the strike price of the option.

bear   Anyone who takes a pessimistic view of the forthcoming long-term trend in a market; that is, one who thinks that a market is, or soon will be, in a long-term downtrend.

bear market   A long-term downtrend (a downtrend lasting months to years) in any market, especially in the stock market, characterized by lower intermediate lows interrupted by lower intermediate highs.

bid   An indication by an investor, trader, or dealer of a willingness to buy a security or a commodity at a certain price; also, the highest current such indication for a specific stock or commodity at any point.

bid and ask   The current quote or quotation on the floor of any market exchange for a specific stock or commodity.

block   A large amount of specific stock, generally 10,000 or more shares.

blue chip   The common stock of an established industry leader whose products or services are widely known and that has a solid record of performance in both good and bad economic environments.

book value   A measure of the net worth of a share of common stock.

bottom   The lowest price within a market movement that occurs before the trend changes and starts moving up.

break   A downward price movement that goes below previous important lows and continues to carry downward.

breakout   An upward price movement that goes above previous important highs and continues to carry upward.

bull   Anyone who takes an optimistic view of the forthcoming long-term trend in a market; that is, one who thinks that a market is, or soon will be, in a long-term uptrend.

bull market   A long-term price movement in any market characterized by a series of higher intermediate highs interrupted by higher consecutive intermediate lows.

commission   The fee charged to a client by a registered broker for the execution of an order to buy or sell a stock, bond, commodity, option, or the like.

correction   An intermediate market price movement that moves contrary to the long-term trend.

Dow Jones Industrial Average (DJIA)   The most widely used indicator of market activity, composed of an average of 30 large issues within the industrial sector of the economy.

Dow Jones Transportation Average (TRAN)   The most widely reported indicator of stock activity in the transportation sector of the economy, composed of an average of 20 large issues.

Dow Jones Utility Average (UTIL)   The most widely reported indicator of stock activity in the utility sector composed of 15 gas, electric, and power company issues.

earnings   The net income available for common stock divided by the number of shares outstanding, reported quarterly by most companies (also earnings-per-share).

floor trader   A member of an exchange who enters transactions for his or her own account from the floor of the exchange; synonymous with local trader.

glamour stock   A favored, highly traded stock, usually of an established company that has performed well and paid dividends in good times and bad.

growth stock   A relatively speculative stock, usually one of a relatively new company that is expected to grow at a fast rate.

high   The highest price a security or commodity reaches within a specified time period.

index futures   Futures contracts traded on the basis of an underlying cash index or average.

long-term trend   Price movements tending to be generally up or generally down and lasting over a period of months to years.

low   The lowest price of a security or commodity reached during a specific time period.

margin   The amount of equity (cash) as a percentage of market value of the underlying market interest held in a margin account.

offer   An indication by a trader or investor of a willingness to sell a security or a commodity; or, in a quote, the current lowest price at which anyone is willing to sell a security or commodity.

over-the-counter (OTC) market   A market of traded stocks that are not listed on the major exhanges.

quote   The current bid and offer for a security on the floor of the exchange on which it is traded.

resistance   Any price level that is deemed a significant high in trading by the market and offers a place to sell the market.

S&P futures   A futures index traded on the basis of the S&P 500 cash index.

stop order   An order given to a broker that becomes a market order when the market price of the underlying instrument reaches or exceeds the specific price stated in the stop order.

support   Any price level deemed a significant low in trading by the market and that offers a place to buy the market.

technical analysis   A method of market forecasting that relies exclusively on the study of past price and volume behavior to predict future price movements.

volume   The number of shares of stocks that change ownership in a given time period.

For Further Reading

Abell, Howard. *The Day Trader's Advantage: How to Move from One Winning Position to the Next.* Chicago: Dearborn Financial Publishing, 1997.

——. *Risk Reward: The Art and Science of Successful Trading.* Chicago: Dearborn Financial Publishing, 1998.

Barach, Roland. *Mindtraps: Mastering the Inner World of Investing.* Homewood, Ill.: Dow Jones-Irwin, 1988.

Baruch, Bernard M. *Baruch: My Own Story.* New York: Holt, Rinehart & Winston, 1957.

Douglas, Mark. *The Disciplined Trader.* New York: New York Institute of Finance, 1990.

Eng, William F. *The Day Trader's Manual: Theory, Art, and Science of Profitable Short-Term Investing.* New York: John Wiley, 1993.

——. *Trading Rules: Strategies for Success.* Chicago: Dearborn Financial Publishing, 1990.

Friedfertig, Marc, and George West. *The Electronic Day Trader.* New York: McGraw Hill, 1998.

Gann, W.D. *How to Make Profits Trading in Commodities.* Pomeroy: Lambert-Gann, 1976.

Houtkin, Harvey, and David Waldman. *Secret of the SOES Bandit.* New York: McGraw Hill, 1998.

Koppel, Robert. *Bulls, Bears, and Millionaires: War Stories of the Trading Life.* Chicago: Dearborn Financial Publishing, 1997.

——. *The Intuitive Trader: Developing Your Inner Market Wisdom.* New York: John Wiley, 1996.

261

————. *The Tao of Trading*. Chicago: Dearborn Financial Publishing, 1997.

Koppel, Robert, and Howard Abell. *The Innergame of Trading: Modeling the Psychology of the Top Traders*. New York: McGraw Hill, 1993.

————. *The Outer Game of Trading: Modeling the Trading Strategies of Today's Market Wizards*. New York: McGraw Hill, 1994.

Le Bon, Gustave. *The Crowd: A Study of the Popular Mind*, 2d ed. Atlanta: Cherokee, 1982.

Schwager, Jack D. *Market Wizards: Interviews with Top Traders*. New York: New York Institute of Finance, 1989.

————. *The New Market Wizards: Conversations with America's Top Traders*. New York: Harper Business, 1992.

Schwartz, Martin. *Pit Bull: Lessons from Wall Street's Champion Trader*. New York: Harper Business, 1998.

Sperandeo, Victor, with Brown T. Sullivan. *Trader Vic—Methods of a Wall Street Master*. New York: John Wiley, 1991.

Index

About the Author

Howard Abell is chief operating officer of the Innergame Division of Rand Financial Services, Inc., concentrating on brokerage and execution services for institutional and professional traders. Abell is the coauthor, with Bob Koppel, of *The Innergame of Trading* (McGraw-Hill, 1993) and *The Outer Game of Trading* (McGraw-Hill, 1994). He is the author of *The Day Trader's Advantage* (Dearborn, 1996), *Spread Trading* (Dearborn, 1997), and *Risk Reward* (Dearborn, 1998). Abell currently manages Tao Partners. He actively day trades stocks and futures.

For additional information about financial seminars or services, please contact Howard Abell:

Innergame Division/Rand Financial Services, Inc.
Chicago Mercantile Exchange
30 South Wacker Drive, Suite 2200
Chicago, IL 60606
800-726-3088
Fax: 312-559-8848
E-mail: hma@innergame.com